Advance Praise for *Beyond the Instant*

"A fine and timely read! Written with passion and empathy, Rabbi Wildes' important book urges young Jews around the world not just to treasure their heritage and history but to recognize why Judaism's timeless values have much to say in today's complex world."

—**Rabbi Lord Jonathan Sacks**, former Chief Rabbi of the United Hebrew Congregations of the Commonwealth

"Rabbi Mark Wildes has demonstrated a unique ability to reach out to Jews of all backgrounds and help them find the beauty and relevance of Judaism to their lives. He is a kind of Pied Piper to scores of millennials who gravitate to him on the Upper West Side of Manhattan. This book reflects his wisdom and his kindness. It demonstrates why so many Jews look to him as their 'rabbi.'"

—**Deborah E. Lipstadt**, author of *Denying the Holocaust* and Dorot Professor of Modern Jewish and Holocaust Studies, Emory University

"In *Beyond the Instant: Jewish Wisdom for Lasting Happiness in a Fast-Paced, Social Media World*, Rabbi Mark Wildes has written a highly readable book with practical advice rooted in the wisdom of religion and ancient writings. Using multiple examples from a wide array of sources, both contemporary and biblical, Rabbi Wildes addresses the pressing questions of our times: the path to enduring happiness, what matters in looking for a life-partner and how to achieve mindfulness in a world filled with distraction and the superficial. I strongly recommend this book to anybody who is interested in achieving a fresh perspective grounded in the deep knowledge that Judaism has imparted to the world over the millennia."

—**Dr. David Pelcovitz**, Straus Chair in Psychology and Education, Azrieli Graduate School, Yeshiva University

"Rabbi Mark Wildes has inspired thousands of young women and men in the last two decades to take their Judaism more seriously through his innovative programs, meaningful services, and exciting classes at the

Manhattan Jewish Experience (MJE) that he founded and leads. With this excellent book, he now brings his message to an even wider audience who will benefit from his deep wisdom and insight. Blessed with prodigious learning and vast outreach experience, Rabbi Wildes beautifully demonstrates how the age-old wisdom of the Torah is directly relevant to the core issues of twenty-first century living. Clearly written, thoughtful, learned, and practical, this is a book that will interest, challenge and educate novice and old-timer alike."

—**Rabbi Jacob J. Schacter**, professor of Jewish History and Jewish Thought and Senior Scholar, Center for the Jewish Future, Yeshiva University

"Mark Wildes is a living legend. His success in demonstrating to countless modern-day Jews the relevance, the beauty and the joys of our ancient faith are unparalleled—and the secrets of how he managed to transform so many lives are revealed in this treasure house of wisdom and inspiration."

—**Rabbi Benjamin Blech**, Professor of Talmud, Yeshiva University

"*Beyond the Instant* is like reading all of Malcolm Gladwell's books, except this will not only better your life, it will actually nourish your soul. It's not just self-help. It's self-fulfillment."

—**Elon Gold**, comedian, actor, writer, and producer

"From Maimonides to *The Matrix*, Wildes shows an impressive ability to seamlessly fuse Torah teachings with pop culture in a manner that makes for an accessible, entertaining, and insightful read."

—*The Algemeiner*

"Finally . . . a Jewish take on wisdom to live by."

—*Publishers Weekly*

"[Rabbi Wildes] does not cast guilt—but instead elucidates on the beneficial effects of following various commandments and practices."

—*San Diego Jewish World*

Beyond

THE

INSTANT

Beyond
THE
INSTANT

Jewish Wisdom for Lasting Happiness in a Fast-Paced, Social Media World

Rabbi Mark Wildes

Skyhorse Publishing

All rights reserved. No part of this book may be reproduced in any manner without the express written consent of the publisher, except in the case of brief excerpts in critical reviews or articles. All inquiries should be addressed to Skyhorse Publishing, 307 West 36th Street, 11th Floor, New York, NY 10018.

Skyhorse Publishing books may be purchased in bulk at special discounts for sales promotion, corporate gifts, fund-raising, or educational purposes. Special editions can also be created to specifications. For details, contact the Special Sales Department, Skyhorse Publishing, 307 West 36th Street, 11th Floor, New York, NY 10018 or info@skyhorsepublishing.com.

Skyhorse® and Skyhorse Publishing® are registered trademarks of Skyhorse Publishing, Inc.®, a Delaware corporation.

Visit our website at www.skyhorsepublishing.com.

10 9 8 7 6 5 4 3 2 1

Library of Congress Cataloging-in-Publication Data is available on file.

Cover design by Michelle Soffen

Print ISBN: 978-1-5107-3185-1
Ebook ISBN: 978-1-5107-3186-8

Printed in the United States of America

CONTENTS

ACKNOWLEDGMENTS

I am privileged to have been blessed with mentors, family members, and friends who have inspired me in my work and without whom this book could never have been written.

Although it has been over twenty years since her passing, my mother, Ruth B. Wildes, of blessed memory, showed me the kind of love and encouragement which nurtures me to this day. My mother was a person of great religious devotion and my first genuine source of spiritual inspiration. Her love for the Shabbat and graciousness with which she received both friends and strangers at her expanding Shabbat table inspired me to establish MJE and to dedicate its outreach work to her memory. This book is a testament to the love she gave me and the model of Judaism she created in our home.

My father, may he continue to live and be well, remains my greatest mentor. From grade school through graduate school my father would correct all the mistakes in my papers with his notorious red pen. It was sometimes a brutal experience but he taught me how to write and speak, reviewing my sermons to this day. My professor in law school and my chavruta, my study partner, my father is someone from whom I continue to learn and with whom I am privileged to study Torah. He has stood behind my every endeavor and fully supported my decision to establish MJE and devote myself to education and outreach. This book is therefore a tribute to my father, my teacher.

Jill, my partner for the last twenty-two years, is my greatest inspiration. I had the privilege of watching her grow into an observant Jew and her love and passion for Torah and Jewish life has inspired hundreds of others to explore their own spiritual heritage. Jill is the ultimate role model to our children and she is the love of my life. She is my constant support while always challenging me to be better. She is my greatest gift, without whom neither MJE nor this book could ever be possible.

My children Yosef, Ezra, Yehuda, and Avigayil are my greatest source of pride, and I wish to acknowledge their love and support in all I do. Special thanks to my two older sons, Yosef and Ezra, for their insights, some of which have been incorporated into this book, and for pushing me to complete this important task.

To my brother Michael, who to this day looks after me like a true older brother. We have always taken pride in each others' accomplishments. Michael's support and that of my sister-in-law Amy mean the world to me.

I wish to offer special thanks to my beloved teacher, Rabbi Dr. Jacob J. Schacter, for reviewing this manuscript and sharing his brilliant insights. For over twenty years I've sat at the feet of this great scholar and noted author, absorbing his extraordinary wisdom and being the recipient of his loving guidance and mentorship. In August of 1998 Rabbi Schacter helped establish MJE at the Jewish Center on the upper West Side of Manhattan, where it remains to this day. He has been there for me and the needs of the organization since day one. This book is just one of the many things for which Rabbi Schacter can take credit.

I wish to acknowledge another beloved mentor, Rabbi Joseph Grunblatt, of blessed memory. Rabbi Grunblatt was my family's rabbi in Forest Hills, Queens, where I grew up. As a child, I always loved Rabbi Grunblatt but it wasn't until I was older that I began to realize the enormity of his scholarship and wisdom. He was also an extraordinary orator with profound depth and substance. Rabbi Grunblatt supported and guided me in my first outreach endeavor at the Queens Jewish Center. May the words of Torah in the pages that follow serve as an elevation for his holy soul.

I wish to also acknowledge past president of Yeshiva University Rabbi

Dr. Norman Lamm, may he continue to live and be well. Considered one of the foremost Jewish thinkers of the last century, Rabbi Lamm has helped guide me and the organization in many important ways. The year-long Lamm Fellowship Program, MJE's most important educational program, proudly bears his name.

I also wish to thank Rabbi Ephraim Buchwald of the National Jewish Outreach Program for inspiring me to create my very first Beginners service, inspiring my wife to begin exploring her Judaism, and supporting me in my outreach work. Thank you as well to Rabbi Haskel Lookstein of Congregation Kehilath Jeshurun for his mentorship and support over the years, as well as to my dear friend, Yeshiva University President Rabbi Ari Berman.

To my MJE colleagues, rabbis Jonathan Feldman, Pinny Rosenthal, and Ezra Cohen, with whom I have worked for almost 20 years. I thank them and my other MJE colleagues as well MJE's Board of Directors for partnering with me in our critical outreach work. Special thanks to Michelle Soffen for her critical help in partnering with Skyhorse Publishing and for her insights into the title, cover design and overall messaging of the book as well as to Herb Schaffner for his wonderful ideas and editing.

As the Hebrew expression goes, *acharon acharon chaviv*, "last, last and beloved," I wish to thank my dear friend George Rohr for his critical help in making this book possible. I have always believed the Almighty sends angels, special individuals who possess the unique ability to inspire others to reach their own potential, enabling them to help others reach their spiritual goals. George has been that force in my life. He dreamed with me in creating MJE almost twenty years ago and has remained an indispensable guide and support in growing the organization ever since, including the writing of this book. He is a living personification of the rabbinic adage "speak little and do much," using his considerable talent to motivate others to reach out and share the beauty and wisdom of Judaism. In the merit of all the love and support George has shown me and so many others, may he and his very special family be blessed with many years of good health, happiness, and success.

INTRODUCTION

One of my students, David, a young practicing attorney living in Manhattan, was in therapy from the time he graduated college until he was twenty-nine. A friend brought him to the Manhattan Jewish Experience (MJE)* for purely social reasons—so he could meet others in the community—but David gravitated to my classes and eventually became one of my most devoted students. As David became more learned in his religious faith, applying the spiritual values he was studying to his own life, many of the issues he had been discussing with his therapist didn't seem to be as significant anymore. He thought it might be a good time to move on, but he would of course need to first discuss this with his therapist, since "all major life decisions needed to cleared by her."

David sat down and turned to his therapist. "I want to thank you for your help over the years," he said. "Your advice has opened my mind and led me to see new alternatives. The one I am now pursuing is my religious faith. In it I have discovered a whole new world of ideas and values that are giving me guidance and really making me happy, so this will be my last session."

The therapist sat back in her chair and stared back at David with one of those looks to which he'd become accustomed over the years. It was

* A not-for-profit organization I founded to engage unaffiliated/less affiliated young Jewish men and women in Jewish life.

a look which was usually followed by some great insight. The therapist leaned forward, smiled, and said, "David, I'm so glad you brought this up. Now we can both see how sick you really are."

True story.

While this incident is certainly not reflective of most therapists, it does demonstrate the prevailing opinion many today have of religious life. We're turned off to religion and so we ignore its teachings. Whether it's all the blood spilled in the name of religious faith, the perception some have of God as angry and punishing, or the now widely held belief in relative morality, religion—and anything associated with it—is seen as primitive, backward, or just irrelevant. As such, religious teachings have become the *last* place people will look to find the kind of meaning, purpose, and direction so many are seeking in their lives today. There are of course other sources and places to find this kind of life direction. From our therapists to what we study in school to where we work to the apps on our phones. These choices can be exciting—but how many of them produce long term satisfaction, *beyond the instant?*

Advances in science and technology have given us opportunities and conveniences of which our grandparents could have only dreamed. Information is instantaneously available to us at our fingertips. Communication with people anywhere and everywhere, as well as traveling across the world, have become commonplace. This technology and information revolution has made our world smaller and so much easier to navigate. Diseases to which previous generations succumbed have been cured, and people are living longer and healthier than ever before. The typical Westerner lives a life of relative affluence, and yet most recent studies confirm we are less happy.

Despite all the benefits we have received from these advances; despite our ability to freely choose from countless options for our lives; despite the easy access we have to ideas and philosophies both old and contemporary; despite our ability to know more about each other and to easily be in contact with one another—our generation is starving for a sense of connectedness and a lasting value system like no generation before.

The instantaneous nature of our world has paradoxically deprived us of the very activities and lifestyle that produce dedication and loyalty, values necessary for sustaining meaningful relationships. There are no longer constraints on the kind of mate we choose or how we date and pursue relationships. Moral relativism, now religiously taught on college campuses, has left us on our own in terms of how we make ethical decisions. In the end, we do what feels right to us or simply adopt the ever-changing mores of our society, but both leave us questioning whether our lives have any real guiding principles. We don't want to be told what to do or what to believe in, but the sensitive among us know something is missing.

We are proud of the freedoms we enjoy and are privileged to live in an open society, but because we lack a higher wisdom to tap into for moral and spiritual direction, we feel trapped. We're trapped in the open with too many options, the only guiding value being our freedom to choose. But *what* should we choose? What are the values and principles that will truly fill our lives with purpose and meaning, and enable us to lead happier and more fulfilled lives?

Too many of us have relegated the wisdom of our religious faith to the past and locked it away. We view the Bible as a relic, an antiquated artifact that loses its relevance after one's Confirmation or Bar/Bat-Mitzvah. I have spent the last twenty years reconnecting young men and women to the teachings of the Hebrew Bible and the Jewish Sages, and I have devoted myself to this enterprise because I believe these works provide timeless wisdom for the very issues young people, and really all of us, struggle with in our contemporary society. It's a unique kind of spiritual wisdom which brings about happiness *beyond the instant*, which can help sustain relationships for the long run. It's an approach that I've seen build confidence, character, and sense of self like nothing else can.

To me, no system of thought and action is more relevant and helpful to the issues and challenges facing Americans and Westerners than the philosophy and heritage of Judaism. Nothing speaks more to the modern issues of consumerism, materialism, lack of meaning, and fulfillment then does the Hebrew Bible and the wisdom of the Jewish Sages. Their principles and values can afford modern men and women not simply a way to worship, but a way to *live*.

This book represents my humble attempt to demonstrate how much contemporary relevance there is to Judaism and, ultimately, how its teachings, if studied and applied, can fill our lives with the kind of purpose and meaning so many of us seek. I have been privileged to personally witness the transformative impact Jewish thought has on people, and how its profound insight and wisdom give the kind of meaning and direction so many young people are looking for today.

Ours is a generation skeptical of religion. Its teachings are viewed as primitive and outdated, and so we've turned to psychology and works of self-help to find a guide. There is certainly wisdom to be found there, but why not also consult a system that has withstood the test of time and from which the great monotheistic faiths have emerged? Why let our religious cynicism deny us a perspective that has provided meaning and direction for billions of people for close to four millennia?

Look at Adam Neumann, founder of WeWork, one of the top startup companies (worth twenty billion dollars), who attributes his happiness not to his financial success, but to his turn to Sabbath observance. Mayim Bialik, the Emmy Award-winning actress on *The Big Bang Theory* (the highest ranked comedy on TV), blogs about how Jewish values and observances bring great meaning to her life. Finally, Senator Joseph Lieberman, nominated by Al Gore for vice president in 2000, consults with rabbis and Jewish scholars for spiritual guidance on the most pressing issues of his life. These high-profile individuals have found personal fulfillment and greater professional success by accessing the wisdom of the Torah, and so can you.

Mining the wisdom of the world's oldest monotheistic faith, this book will confront happiness and relationship issues and answer the following questions:

- What produces true joy and happiness?

- What should we be looking for in a potential spouse?
- Once we've found that person, how can we make the relationship last?
- What is sex really supposed to be about?
- How can I start accepting responsibility and stop shifting the blame?
- How can we learn from our failures?
- How can we take more control of our lives?
- Do you have a mission in life?
- How do we choose values over popularity?
- How can we be more present to enjoy life more?
- Is change really possible?

Chapter 1

HAPPINESS

First Commandment: *Thou Shalt Give*

I often think of my grandfather when I'm asked questions about happiness. At the age of twenty, he fled Bialystok, Poland, and the pogroms that made life unbearable for Jews during the nineteenth and early twentieth centuries. My grandfather, Harry—or as we called him, Zaide (Yiddish for grandfather)—married Sarah and settled in a small town called Olyphant near Scranton, Pennsylvania. Like the other Jews in town, they owned a dry goods store. He also peddled goods door to door, had very little money, smoked a cigar, and enjoyed a schnapps after morning synagogue.

When I visited my Zaide in the store, I almost never saw customers. He could always be found studying Talmud in the back room. Whenever he would see me or call on the phone, the first thing he said was always: "which part of the Talmud did you study today?" Then he'd pepper me with questions.

As a proud *Litvak* (Jew from Lithuania), he suffered no anxiety about living in a state of truth, and sometimes brutal honesty, with others. When a bank error resulted in a tidy sum of money for the synagogue of which he was the treasurer, he insisted the synagogue return every penny.

He thought that Jewish stores in Olyphant should close on the Sabbath (in accordance with Jewish law) despite the loss of income this would mean. His happiness was found in his scholarship, piety, family, and his love for all people.

At my oldest son's Bar-Mitzvah, my father, who is an immigration attorney, shared the following story. Years ago when my Zaide was alive, my father got a call from a colleague in Washington named Ginsberg. Ginsberg said his grandchildren, who lived in Israel, were eligible for citizenship in the United States and he wanted to have them sworn in, but to bring them to America they would need an appointment with an immigration officer.

Ginsberg called my father asking if he could somehow manage to get that appointment within a few weeks so they could spend the holiday of Passover together—otherwise the family would have to be apart for the holiday. My father knew that it takes a year, sometimes more, to get an appointment with the Immigration and Naturalization Service (INS), but he figured he'd try.

After ringing the INS, the only person my father could get on the line was someone by the name of Inspector Kowalchick, in charge of deportation matters. Kowalchick told my father that he worked in deportation and had nothing to do with citizenship. My father thanked him for his time, but before getting off the phone, he asked, "Are you by chance from Olyphant? I vaguely remember a Kowalchick from Olyphant."

Kowalchick answered, "Yes, that's where I grew up. My mother still lives there."

"Well," continued my father, "maybe you can help out a guy from Olyphant?"

Kowalchick replied, "Let me see what I can do."

The next week my father got a call from Kowalchick. "Are you related to Harry Wildes?" he asked.

My father responded, "Yes, that's my father."

"Harry Wildes," Kowalchick said, "the honest Jew. I spoke with my mother and she told me that for years she bought from a Jewish peddler by the name of Harry Wildes. One time she bought a housecoat from him for $1.98 and gave him a twenty-dollar bill and your father gave her the change. That night, around midnight, there was a knock at my mother's door. It was Harry. He had gone a long way to hand my mother a ten-dollar bill, a lot of money in those days. He realized he hadn't given her the right change. She checked and saw he was correct."

The next week my father got an elated call from his client, Ginsberg in Washington. "How did you do it?' he asked my dad.

"How did I do what"?

"We just got notice from the INS that our grandchildren's citizenship interviews are scheduled for next week! How did you manage to pull that off?" asked Ginsberg.

"My father was an honest man," my father answered. "I guess that's something no one forgets."

On my Zaide's tombstone is engraved this rabbinic adage: "Who is wealthy? He who is satisfied with his lot."[1] Although my Zaide was the poorest man I have ever known, he was also the happiest and most content.

In an interesting coincidence, Olyphant is not far from Roseto, Pennsylvania, the location of another remarkable true story about the nature of happiness. The story began in the 1950s. Dr. Stewart Wolf, head of the University of Oklahoma's Department of Medicine, after delivering a medical talk in the small town of Roseto, Pennsylvania, was having a beer with one of the local doctors. The doctor told Wolf that in his seventeen years of practicing medicine in Roseto, he rarely found anyone under the age of sixty-five with heart disease. Dr. Wolf was in shock. This was the 1950s, when heart attacks were an epidemic in America. Wolf called in some of his colleagues and medical students from the university and began an extensive study of the people of Roseto. They went house to house speaking to everyone over the age of twenty-one. The researchers took blood samples, brought in sociologists, and conducted a thorough investigation of the entire population.[2]

3

The results of the study were fascinating. They discovered that in Roseto, most people lived until a ripe old age. No one under fifty-five had died of a heart attack or showed any signs of heart disease, and for men over sixty-five, the death rate from heart disease was roughly half of the rest of the country. Early, sudden, or premature death was virtually unheard of in Roseto, and in the 1950s, years before cholesterol-lowering drugs, there was almost no heart disease in Roseto. There was also no suicide, no alcoholism, no drug addiction, and very little crime. No one in Roseto was on welfare.

Further, the people of Roseto shared the same unhealthy dieting and exercise habits of the surrounding towns. Dieticians discovered that a whopping 41 percent of the people's caloric intake was from fat (they regularly cooked with lard). Hardly anyone exercised. No one did yoga or jogged every day. In fact, many of those who lived in Roseto smoked heavily and struggled with obesity. Yet the death rate in Roseto from heart disease was half the national rate! What accounted for Roseto's longer life span and lower rates of suicide, crime, and alcoholism?

Positive Psychologist[*] Tal Ben-Shahar's course on happiness was the most popular course ever offered at Harvard University. At least a hundred other American universities offer similar courses today. In 2008, publishers produced over four thousand books written about happiness (compared to fifty in 2000).[3] Yet happiness seems to elude our generation. Study after study reveals that Americans consider themselves less happy today than ever before. We have grown sadder and more anxious during the same years that the happiness movement flourished.

The generations of Americans born after 1990 are seeking happiness with greater focus and fervor than others before them. I meet and know many of these young people—they are my friends and my students. They come to MJE and I speak with them about their lives. It seems

---

[*] Positive psychology is the scientific study of the strengths that enable individuals and communities to thrive. The field is founded on the belief that people want to lead meaningful and fulfilling lives, to cultivate what is best within themselves, and to enhance their experiences of love, work, and play.

for many, the more they seek happiness, the more they struggle. They're not alone.

Although we enjoy a standard of living unimaginable to our great-grandparents, there are more stress-related illnesses in America than ever before. The United States, which is among the most affluent and prosperous countries, is the second highest consumer of the world's anti-depressants.[4] Suicide and depression rates have gone up.

One thing is also clear: there is little or no correlation between money and happiness. The research shows that once one has his or her basic needs met, i.e. food and shelter, money and affluence are *not* determining factors of happiness.[5] As one of my psychology teachers, Dr. David Pelcovitz, put it: The man sitting on a public bus on his way to his blue-collar job is no less happy then the man riding on the road beside him, sitting in his chauffeured limousine on the way to his seven-figured salaried position.

Simcha

If money does not make us happy, then what does?

If we look at Hebrew scripture, the Torah, the word for happiness or joy is *simcha*, a word always used in the Hebrew Bible within the context of two other phrases: *and you shall be happy before God*[6] and *you shall be happy in your holiday.*[7] The Torah draws a connection between being in God's presence and celebrating the Jewish holidays, and being in a state of *simcha* or joy.

In ancient times, when the Jewish Temple stood in Jerusalem (the first Temple stood from 832–422 BCE and the second from 516 BCE to 70 CE), one was considered to have been "before God" on the three Jewish festivals—namely Sukkot, Passover, and Shavuot. During each of these festivals, Jewish families would pilgrimage to Jerusalem and bring special offerings in the Temple. The people would come to the Temple, and there they would stand *before God*; in that place and time they would fulfill the command of "and you shall be happy in your holiday."

What created this state of *simcha* or joy on the Festival?

It began with each family making the long and arduous trek to Jerusalem, coming with their offering to the Temple, and it included some other activities, as described by Maimonides, the great philosopher and codifier of Jewish law: *Children should be given roasted seeds, nuts, and sweets. For women, one should buy attractive clothes and jewelry according to one's financial capacity. Men should eat meat and drink wine . . . When a person eats and drinks [in celebration of a holiday], he is obligated to feed converts, orphans, widows, and others who are destitute and poor. In contrast, a person who locks the gates of his courtyard and eats and drinks with his children and his wife, without feeding the poor and the embittered, is [not indulging in] rejoicing associated with a mitzvah, but rather the rejoicing of his belly.*[8]

Thus, to fulfill the biblical command (mitzvah) of rejoicing in the holiday one buys gifts for their family and enjoys good food and drink. Celebrants visiting the Temple must also be careful to share some of the bounty with converts, orphans, and widows—the poor and embittered. The holiday only becomes a mitzvah of joy when one's good fortune is shared with others, specifically with those who may be lacking or on the sidelines.

How do these activities somehow result in achieving a state of *simcha* or joy?

It appears that as far as Judaism is concerned, happiness is created by extending ourselves for *others,* not for ourselves. In contrast, so much of what our generation does to make ourselves happy seems to revolve around *our* inner contentment, not our shared responsibility. We book a vacation. We sign up for a yoga class. We pamper ourselves with a massage or we do something else that makes us feel like we are paying more attention to "me." No doubt these activities reduce stress and provide some semblance of joy, but taking a cue from Maimonides and classical Judaism, these activities produce *pleasure,* not happiness, and pleasure is fleeting.

This may sound like a superficial example, but I've always liked ties, and over the years, whenever I get down, I tend to buy more of them. As part of my work at MJE I do a fair measure of fund-raising, and when I get turned down by a prospective donor I find myself wandering into a clothing store or purchasing a tie from a vendor on the street. Although I'm a decent fund-raiser, I've amassed quite a collection! The whole thing is ridiculous, but that quick purchase does something positive for me; yet I know it's just pleasure—not happiness—and so the feeling quickly fades. Happiness that will last can only come from *giving* to others and from getting *out* of ourselves.

The activities Maimonides delineated as ways to fulfill the biblical command of "being happy in your holiday" all have one thing in common: they are all behaviors which remove us from the natural focus we have upon ourselves, and instead involve us in activities which bind us to God and to other people, and ultimately create a sense of community. The trek to Jerusalem, buying gifts for one's family, and sharing one's bounty with the less fortunate, all shift the focus from *me* to the other, and *that* creates *simcha* or joy.

Scientific studies tell us the very same thing. We benefit neurologically from giving and helping others. The research shows that generosity, both volunteering and giving charity, benefits people of all ages both physically and psychologically: "The benefits of giving are significant, according to those studies: lower blood pressure, lower risk of dementia, less anxiety and depression, reduced cardiovascular risk, and overall greater happiness."[9]

Studies demonstrate that when we think about helping others, we activate a part of the brain called the mesolimbic pathway, which is responsible for feelings of gratification. Helping others releases happiness chemicals like dopamine, an endorphin that blocks pain signals, and oxytocin, otherwise known as the tranquility hormone. Research shows that even just the *thought* of giving money to a specific charity has this effect on the brain.

Most importantly, doing for others helps produce long-term happiness *beyond the instant*. Intuition may tell us that giving to ourselves is the best way to be happy, But that's not the case, according to Dan Ariely, professor of Behavioral Economics and Psychology at Duke University: "If you are a recipient of a good deed, you may have momentary happiness, but your long-term happiness is higher if you are the giver."[10]

An online national survey of 4,500 American adults found that people who volunteer have less trouble sleeping, less anxiety, less helplessness and hopelessness, better friendships and social networks, and a sense of control over chronic conditions.[11]

Science is demonstrating what Jewish tradition has taught for centuries: *lasting* happiness results from giving, and creates a life in which our attention is turned from the "me" to the "you." The Torah teaches us that there is a relationship between being in a state of joy and being "before God." Since God is the ultimate "other," coming before the Almighty forces us to ask ourselves: What have we done for others? Am I living a life of purpose and meaning? Am I simply looking out for myself or am I also concerned for the stranger, the widow, and the orphan? Am I sufficiently connected to others and do I matter enough to other people?

Have I become so absorbed with my own issues?

The late and great Lubavitcher Rebbe, Rabbi Menachem Schneerson, once received a very sad letter from one of his followers which went something like this: "I would like the Rebbe's help. I wake up each day sad and apprehensive. I can't concentrate. I find it hard to pray. I keep the commandments but find no spiritual satisfaction. I go to synagogue but feel alone. I begin to wonder what life is about. I need help." The Rebbe wrote a brilliant reply, which didn't contain a single new word. He merely circled the first word of each sentence from his student's letter and then sent the letter back. The first word of each sentence was the letter "I."

That was the young man's problem. It was all about him.

Former Chief Rabbi of England Lord Jonathan Sacks pointed out that there is only one book in the entire Hebrew Bible that uses the first-person singular "I" and that is *Sefer Kohelet*, King Solomon's Book of Ecclesiastes: "I built for myself, I planted for myself, I acquired for myself," said Solomon. No other book in Hebrew scripture uses "I" so many times, but that was Solomon's problem: he kept thinking about himself. He was brilliant, rich, and powerful, but he was not happy. [12]

The Roseto Code

When researchers started digging deeper into the small rural town of Roseto, Pennsylvania, to discover why people's life spans were significantly longer, why there was no suicide, and no drug or alcohol problems like in so many other parts of the country, they learned that Roseto was settled by a group of immigrants from Southern Italy in the late 1800s. These immigrants shared a common faith, family, culture, and memories. This created a particularly close-knit community.

Almost everyone in Roseto attended Mass each Sunday. They volunteered. Researchers counted twenty-two separate civic organizations in a town with a population of less than two thousand. They exhibited a strong sense of responsibility of one person to the next. The senior citizens used to sit on their rockers on their front porches and if a kid was caught cutting school, an older person would drag him to the principal's office. The researchers noticed how townsfolk stopped to chat with one another in Italian on the street corner and how they cooked for each other in their backyards. They saw how many homes had three generations living under one roof, and how much respect grandparents commanded.

Then something changed. In the 1970s, as the new generation tried to become more Americanized, they started to reject the old Italian folkways. They changed the architecture of their homes, and so instead of front porches they put in two-car garages. Now, as in other parts of the country, people could live and die without ever knowing their neighbors, besides maybe saying hello. Religious participation went down. Volunteering decreased. People began to spend more time on their own issues, and today Roseto's heart attack rate has more than doubled and equals the national average.[13]

These trends have unfolded across our entire society during the past forty years. Harvard political scientist Robert Putnam published his landmark book, *Bowling Alone*, in 1999, which identified a national decline in civic engagement. Drawing on nearly 500,000 interviews, Putnam showed that from the 1970s to the 1990s, people signed fewer petitions, belonged to fewer organizations, knew their neighbors less, met with friends less frequently, and even socialized with family less often. There was a marked decline in attendance at religious services and civic organizations, and even though more Americans were bowling than ever, fewer were joining teams. More were bowling alone.[14]

The rise of social and political clustering on the Internet has intensified this atomization and made it harder for us to get out of ourselves and become part of a larger supportive team. There are, of course, other factors which produce happiness, like being more grateful and having lower expectations, but existentially if we want to be happy, we need to live as part of a community where individuals care about one another. This is one of the reasons so many young urbanites living active but somewhat isolated lives in big cities are unhappy. There isn't that sense that we matter enough to other people, that we live among others who care for us, or for whom we care.

The story of Roseto shows that we need to volunteer for causes in which we believe, attend religious services so we can connect with something greater than ourselves, and *give* to other people. As my esteemed teacher, former president of Yeshiva University Rabbi Dr. Norman Lamm, once said in a sermon: "The more concerned we are with our own happiness, the less likely we are to achieve it. But the Sages in Ethics of our Fathers teach: 'if I am for myself, who am I?' The true *simcha* (happiness) is attained only when I lose myself, only when my concern is with making others happy. That's why the mitzvah of *simcha* in the Torah is coupled with the mitzvah to provide joy for the poor, for the widow and for the orphan. To be happy we have to stop trying to make *ourselves* happy and start by taking care of others. That will bring true happiness."[15]

This helps explain a comment by Maimonides with respect to the Jewish holiday of Purim. To celebrate the day of Purim, one is supposed to give gifts to the poor, send food baskets to one's friends and neighbors, and enjoy a festive meal. Maimonides writes: "Better to increase in gifts to the poor than increasing in the meal or in the sending of food baskets for there is no greater joy and glory than gladdening the heart of poor people, orphans, widows and strangers . . ."[16]

Taking care of other people helps produce long-term happiness precisely because it removes the focus from ourselves and ultimately enables us to live a life of purpose and meaning. The by-product of such a life is a state of happiness.

In a major study of over two thousand individuals from twelve states and forty families over a five-year period, sociologists Christian Smith and Hilary Davidson concluded that the connection between charity, volunteering, and one's state of happiness is unmistakable: "very happy people" averaged volunteering almost ten times more than those who were "unhappy." Their findings also concluded that there were lower rates of depression among Americans who donated more than 10 percent of their incomes: 41 percent say they rarely or never experience depression versus 32 percent for everyone else. In addition, Smith and Davidson found that Americans who are more giving in relationships, who are more emotionally available and hospitable, are more likely to be in excellent health versus those who are not.[17]

Taking care of others isn't just an admirable or selfless thing: it makes us happier and healthier. Much of Jewish tradition is designed to create this kind of existence. The Jewish Sages speak of three pillars of the Jewish faith and of the Jewish home: *Shabbat* (The Sabbath), *Kashrut* (Dietary Laws), and *Taharat Hamishpacha* (Family Purity).

Shabbat demands we rest, but in such a way as to bind us to others and create a sense of community. As the great Hebrew poet Achad Haa'am famously wrote: "More than the Jews have kept the *Shabbat*, the *Shabbat* has kept the Jews."[18] Between the family and communal meals, synagogue services and the overall social nature of the day, this one day each week ensures that people, wherever they may live, are part of a tight knit community.

Kashrut, or the Jewish dietary laws, challenge us to eat, not simply based on what we like, but in accordance with a set of Divine principles so the otherwise mundane activity of eating can be used to connect to something higher than our stomachs.

Finally, *Tahart Hamishpacha*, the laws of family purity, which play a critical role in sexual intimacy, help ensure that the sexual relationship between husband and wife is just as much about satisfying one's partner as oneself.

Not to mention the central role that *chesed*—performing acts of loving kindness—occupies in Jewish life. Jewish tradition challenges one to give a portion of their annual earnings to those less fortunate, to lend money to help friends when they are in need, to make happy a bride and groom on the day of their wedding, to escort the dead, and open one's home to provide hospitality to the stranger. These are the types of giving activities, if practiced with regularity, which ultimately produce happiness.

On a very personal level this is the only way I can understand why I and my colleagues so enjoy the work we do serving the community. On a purely rational level it makes little sense. We devote ourselves endlessly to the needs of other people, often strangers, and in a purely material sense, earn very little in return. But besides the opportunity to spend time with quality people, working to help others produces true joy. It fills me in a way nothing else does, especially that feeling of total exhaustion at the end of a successful program where I feel like I've made a real impact on people's lives. I feel beat up from the exhaustion, but there's just nothing like it. It's the same kind of feeling a parent has when investing in his children, a teacher in his students, or a patriot in his country.

Joseph's Example

I will never forget a man by the name of Joseph Nachmias who spoke to my students one year on our annual trip to Israel. At the tender age of fourteen, Joseph joined the British army (along with thirty thousand other young Jews living in British mandate Palestine) to fight the Germans. Three years later, when he was all of seventeen, Joseph joined the Irgun, the Jewish underground, to fight against the British and create the Jewish State. He told us he had his tooth removed and replaced with a gold one so he could better impersonate Arabs, stealing weapons from the British for the Zionist cause. Joseph was part of a famous operation to break free eight Jewish fighters who were supposed to be hanged by the British.

As I listened to him address our group, I noticed he couldn't help but smile. He had this look of total contentment and happiness, because he lived his life for others. You could see how proud he felt of having helped to create the State of Israel. At the same time, the level of stress Joseph had experienced was huge. Like my grandfather Harry, he enjoyed very little in the way of pleasure, but was filled with happiness and contentment.

We are a composite of body and soul. If we only pursue pleasure, we feed the body but the soul goes hungry and we become unhappy. Money and things may make our bodies feel good—they feed the physical part of who we are—but connecting to God, taking care of one's family, getting ourselves into the world of ideas and the wisdom of Torah, and devoting ourselves to important causes, other people, and their needs feed the soul and place us "before God," which ultimately produces happiness.

Each of us can increase our level of happiness by resolving to do what all the contemporary studies tell us make us happier and what Jewish sources have pointed to for more than three millennia—forge a closer bond with our community, raise our spiritual commitment to feel more connected to our Creator, and do more for those in need. If you're *not* part of a community or volunteering to help someone or working for a cause in which you believe, make that change now. The irony is that the best thing we can do for ourselves is to get *out of ourselves* and do for others. Our levels of happiness increase when we do just the opposite of what we've been trained to do when we want to feel better: help someone else and stay connected to your spiritual source.

There's no crime in pampering yourself. We all need vacations and breaks to unwind and clear our heads. But to be truly happy and find contentment, we need to be devoted to other people, important causes, and spirituality. *Those* are the factors which enable us to live a life of purpose, meaning, and ultimately, happiness.

Notes

1. Ethics of Our Fathers, 4:1.
2. John G. Bruhn and Stewart Wolf, *The Roseto Story* (University of Oklahoma Press, 1979); John G. Bruhn and Stewart Wolf, *The Power of Clan: The Influence of Human Relationships in Heart Disease* (New Brunswick, NJ: Transactions Publishers, 1993).
3. Carlin Flora, "The Pursuit of Happiness," *Psychology Today*, January 1, 2009, https://www.psychologytoday.com/articles/200901/the-pursuit-happiness.
4. Tom Hale, "Which Countries Consume the Most Antidepressants," iflscience.com, November 11, 2013, http://www.iflscience.com/health-and-medicine/which-countries-consume-most-antidepressants/.
5. Jill Suttie, "How Does Valuing Money Affect Your Happiness?" *Greater Good Magazine*, October 30, 2017, https://greatergood.berkeley.edu/article/item/how_does_valuing_money_affect_your_happiness.
6. Deuteronomy 16:11.
7. Deuteronomy 16:14.
8. Maimonides, Mishnah Torah, Laws of the Festivals, Chapter 6, Laws 17 and 18.
9. Terri Yablonsky Stat, "Be Generous: It's a Simple Way to Stay Healthier," *Chicago Tribune*, August 6, 2015, http://www.chicagotribune.com/lifestyles/health/sc-hlth-0812-joy-of-giving-20150806-story.html.
10. Ibid.
11. Megan Kelly, "United Health Care and Volunteer Match Release," Do Good, Live Well Study, adt.volunteermatch.org, July 28, 2010, https://blogs.volunteermatch.org/volunteeringiscsr/2010/07/28/unitedhealthcare-and-volunteermatch-release-do-good-live-well-study/.
12. Rabbi Jonathan Sacks, "The True Path to Inner Happiness," www.rabbisacks.org, February 23, 2003, http://rabbisacks.org/the-true-path-to-inner-happiness-published-in-the-daily-mail/.
13. Kay Cassill, "Stress Has Hit Roseto, Pa., Once the Town Heart Disease Passed By," *People Magazine*, June 16, 1980, http://people.com/archive/stress-has-hit-roseto-pa-once-the-town-heart-disease-passed-by-vol-13-no-24/.
14. Robert Putnam, *Bowling Alone* (New York: Simon and Schuster, 2016).
15. Sermon by Rabbi Dr. Norman Lamm, delivered on October 6, 1966 at the Jewish Center, found on the Lamm Heritage website: http://brussels.mc.yu.edu/gsdl/collect/lammserm/index/assoc/HASH01c3/8231d18e.dir/doc.pdf.

16. Maimonides, Mishna Torah, Laws of Megilah and Chanukah 2:17.
17. Christian Smith and Hilary Davidson, *The Paradox of Generosity: Giving We Receive, Grasping We Lose* (New York: Oxford University Press, 2014).
18. Achad Ha'am/Asher Ginsberg, "Sabbath and Zionism," http://benye huda.org/ginzberg/Gnz051.html.

Chapter 2

LOVE, DATING, AND RELATIONSHIPS

Second Commandment: *Thou Shalt Commit*

In my favorite comedy monologue, Jerry Seinfeld made the following insightful remark:

> Why is commitment such a big problem for a man? I think that for some reason when a man is driving down that freeway of love, the woman he's with is like an exit, but he doesn't want to get off there. He wants to keep driving. And the woman is like, "Look, gas, food, lodging, that's our exit, that's everything we need to be happy . . . Get off here, now!" But the man is focusing on the sign underneath that says, "Next exit twenty-seven miles," and he thinks, "I can make it." Sometimes he can, sometimes he can't. Sometimes, the car ends up on the side of the road, hood up and smoke pouring out of the engine. He's sitting on the curb all alone (mumbling to himself), "I guess I didn't realize how many miles I was racking up."

The image of driving and driving, and never wanting to get off the highway, is a very telling image in our contemporary society. I live and work on Manhattan's Upper West Side, the mecca of Jewish singlehood where a lot of guys are metaphorically sitting on the curb mumbling to themselves.

An article in the *New York Times* showed another side of this issue of commitment among the many twenty- to thirtysomethings of New York City. The article discussed how people are sincerely looking for a relationship, not just a one-night stand, but on the other hand, they value their independence and don't want to settle down or commit to one person on a permanent basis. "It's not that people aren't dating," explained Ms. Rozler, an editorial assistant at Allworth Press when she is not practicing nightclub anthropology. "It's that there's this weird gray area. People still want to be in relationships, but they don't want to be settling."[1]

Are people not settling down because they are scared to make the wrong decision?

When a friend of mine was getting married, just as he was about to walk down the aisle, the officiating rabbi asked him, "Are you sure?" The question took my friend by surprise. He just looked back at the rabbi and said nothing.

The rabbi chuckled and said, "Good, only a fool could be sure."

There's no such thing as certainty when it comes to matters of the heart. We also change as we grow, and so making a commitment to one person requires some faith and a willingness to take a chance. Others simply value their independence too much to settle down.

Whatever the reason, most of us will try to avoid commitment, but how necessary is it for a meaningful and lasting relationship? Is it possible to get that amazing feeling of intimacy, peace, and security that comes from being in a committed relationship without having to commit to one person and settle down?

Adam One

To understand Judaism's approach to making commitments and whether they are necessary to have a sustainable relationship, we need to go back to the very first relationship: Adam and Eve in the Garden of Eden. In a book that profoundly impacted my life, *The Lonely Man of Faith*, the great twentieth-century philosopher and sage, Rabbi Joseph Soloveitchik, referred to by many as "the Rav," explains the two very different ways the Bible describes Adam and Eve's creation. Rabbi Soloveitchik demonstrates how, in chapter one of Genesis, the Torah describes Adam and Eve's creation in one way, and, in chapter two, in quite another way. The book explains how the different descriptions of Adam and Eve's creation reflect the two different aspects of our existence and the resulting conflicting drives.[2]

One of the differences is the way the Bible describes how Adam and Eve first came into the world: In chapter one of Genesis, the Bible says that Adam and Eve were created as one, as a combined form of male and female. As the verse reads: "male and female God created them,"[3] but in chapter two, the Bible says that Adam and Eve were created as separate beings, that Adam was created first and only later did Eve come into the picture.

Well, which is it? Were Adam and Eve created together or separately?

Rabbi Soloveitchik explains that Adam in chapter one, "Adam One," is created together with Eve because that Adam is commanded by God to dominate the environment: "fill the earth and subdue it."[4] Adam One's mission was to harness the forces of nature and build a better world. Since he is focused exclusively on trying to tackle the environment, Adam One is therefore created together with Eve simply because he needs her. As one of Rabbi Soloveitchik's students paraphrased the Rav's words: "His simultaneous creation with Eve reflects his immediate need for a work partner to join him in nature's conquest and mastery."[5] He continued, "Helpless individuals realize they cannot cope with life's multifarious needs and challenges when working alone. Partnerships are formed, contracts are signed and treaties of mutual assistance are made."[6]

Adam and Eve's relationship as described in chapter one is utilitarian and practical. Adam and Eve satisfy each other's needs, but they are not bound to each other emotionally. We all know relationships like this, whether in friendships and even in some marriages, where a couple work well together but they don't connect on a deeper, metaphysical level, and so the relationship is productive, but the couple is not bound existentially and so the relationship never becomes holy.

Whenever I counsel students who wish to be in a relationship, but are not willing to make a commitment to one person, I think about Adam and Eve's relationship as described in chapter one of the Bible—since Adam One approaches Eve with the same attitude. Adam One is created with the drive to dominate the environment and for that he needs Eve.

We too have needs—we have a need for companionship, to be loved and cared for, to have someone with whom we can enjoy a good movie or book—and so naturally we look for others to fill those needs. We need someone to help make us to feel more secure and important, especially if we get sick, have a bad day at work, or something else goes wrong. There is a need to have sex, to be physically intimate, and to have children and pass on one's legacy, all legitimate needs. To fulfill these needs we date. We look for a partner who can fulfill as many of these needs as possible. Seems simple and harmless, right?

Not so simple.

There are two problems with approaching relationships using a purely needs-based approach: first, it's impossible to find *one* person who can fulfill so many diverse needs. Maybe we can find someone to whom we are physically attracted, but intellectual compatibility is just not there. Maybe we can find someone who will be a good parent, but they don't make us laugh. Maybe we can find one person who can satisfy some or even many of these needs, but one person who can fulfill them all? And who we also *like*? Not happening.

The second problem with a needs-oriented approach to relationships is that even if the couple share an intellectual similarity, physical chemistry, and sense of humor, these are all surface needs. The deepest and most pressing need, *the need to feel understood*, may still not be met, even if one finds another with whom one enjoys going to the movies, discussing politics, or having sex. I believe marriages of this kind often end in divorce.

Adam Two

To understand the need to be understood, we must go past Adam One, beyond the way the Bible describes the very practical, power-sharing, and need-oriented relationship of Adam and Eve in chapter one, to Adam and Eve as they are described in chapter two of the book of Genesis. Whereas in chapter one Adam and Eve are created together, in chapter two, Adam is created all alone and Eve emerges later. Adam exists in this state of aloneness for some time until God in the Torah says, " . . . it is not good for man to be alone, I will make for him a helpmate."[7]

Rabbi Soloveitchik says that since this Adam (Adam Two) was created alone, with no companion with whom to communicate, he becomes existentially insecure. He has no other counterpart in the universe, and so he feels completely distinct and isolated. Interestingly, it is in this state that God commands Adam to name all the animals in the Garden of Eden. This naming exercise makes Adam feel even more lonely because he comes to realize that the animals are completely different from him and that he shares nothing in common with them. This causes him to feel even less understood and therefore even more alone.

Naming the animals left Adam feeling like many do after a series of bad dates—alone and misunderstood. Rabbi Soloveitchik explains that what causes people to feel lonely is "the awareness of one's uniqueness and exclusiveness." This is different from being alone. Being alone just means you're not with anyone else. Being *lonely*, on the other hand, says Rabbi Soloveitchik, is "a spiritual human situation."[8] It means not being understood. You can be in Madison Square Garden sitting among thousands of fans at a rock concert and still be "lonely" if there is no one else in that room, or in the world, who truly understands you. Loneliness, says Rabbi Soloveitchik, is "an existential awareness or a metaphysical state not only of the mind but of the soul as well."[9]

Adam realized that there was no other being in the world that was like him, that he could relate to, or that could understand him, and so he felt lonely. This is the very feeling with which every human being is plagued, since each of us is a unique individual, distinct from all other people. The only way to defeat this existential loneliness is by being with someone who understands you, someone who, as the expression goes, "gets you." However, as my friend, Yeshiva University President Rabbi Dr. Ari Berman, once shared with me, this can only happen if you've sufficiently opened yourself to that person, so he or she can understand you and ultimately accept you for who you are. That, he suggested, explains the symbolism of Adam and Eve's nakedness in the Garden of Eden—the idea that they had totally revealed themselves to one another. Honesty of this kind needs a truly committed relationship to flourish. For who is willing to reveal their most intimate secrets to someone who may disclose them to someone else? Who is going to feel safe enough to expose their true selves to another who may reveal their secrets to someone else or who may be "out the door" the next day?

That is why I believe Judaism strongly promotes marriage, because for all its flaws and challenges, marriage creates the highest possible level of commitment so we can feel comfortable sharing and revealing our inner selves, thereby easing our existential separateness and anxiety. This also explains why the biblical term for sex is knowledge: "And Adam knew Eve his wife and she conceived."[10] Sex is another way of *knowing* another, part of the process of revealing oneself within the environment of marriage where it is safe to do so. Otherwise we are forced to hold back, hiding our true selves, and our existential loneliness prevails.

But here's the good news: None of this needs to be fully developed *before* we get married. In our world today, we've somehow convinced ourselves that we must have whatever it is marriage brings before the marriage even starts. But that's what marriage itself is for—giving ourselves the comfort zone to reveal who we are to another person. That's precisely *why* we get married, not the prerequisite.

The one thing necessary to have *before* marriage is a true desire to open ourselves to that person: Do I want this other person to truly know me and do I have a desire to know them? If the answer to that question is yes, then assuming the couple has a physical attraction to one another and possesses shared values and goals, they should get married and spend the rest of their lives finding out about each other, using the safe zone of marriage to reveal their entire selves to one another. That's why sexual intimacy in Judaism *follows* marriage, as sex is just another way of revealing oneself to the other once the commitment has been made.

But as we all know, opening ourselves up is also a way to create a relationship in the first place, and therein lies the "catch-22" of dating. As one of my students once shared with me, "Rabbi, if I'm not in a committed relationship, where I have a certain level of trust, then, by definition, I will be reluctant to open myself up, but if I don't, then my ability to bond and connect with that other person is limited. What should I do?"

Good question! I answered that in dating we must do *some* revealing of our inner selves to get things moving, to create a connection and feel some chemistry, but the ultimate revelation, the true exposure which ultimately enables us to feel understood and accepted, is reserved for marriage where it feels safe to reveal even more.

Naturally there are no guarantees. You can do a lot of the right things and the situation may still not work out. But my advice remains the same: look for someone who understands you and who you will have a desire to get to know on a deeper level. If you find such a person, and you have the same basic values and goals, then stop dating. Go out and buy a ring and propose. (This is primarily being said for the men.) Don't keep on feeling you must continue to reveal more and more of yourself and learn every single nuance about your partner, or that they must know every little thing about you. You have the rest of your life for that.

Our Leg Hurts

This revealing and learning about one's partner is also one of the things which keeps marriage interesting for the long run. As the couple moves through real-life situations, they learn more about the other and what their partner needs to be happy. This deepens the bond, and over time true love develops. Love, according to Jewish thought, is based on giving. The Hebrew word for love is *ahava*—the root of which is *hav*, which means to give. Love develops from giving, which can only happen when each partner truly understands the other and makes their partner feel understood and accepted. This is one of the reasons why *listening* is such an important skill to develop in a marriage (and in any relationship) because listening helps one person feel like the other "gets them" and is willing to do what they can to satisfy their needs. Those needs change over time, but as the levels of knowledge, understanding, and acceptance increase, so does the love and so does their *oneness*. The Talmud says that a man's wife is like a part of his body.[11] The story is told of the great saint of Jerusalem, Rabbi Aryeh Levin, who went with his wife to the doctor when she was suffering from severe pain in her leg. When they arrived at the doctor, who asked what the problem was, the rabbi famously answered, "*our* leg hurts." Oneness is the result of true love and that's the goal of marriage expressed in this famous verse of the Torah: *Therefore should man leave his father and mother and cleave unto his wife and they will be one flesh.*[12] They are one. They have one leg. That's true love and that takes a lifetime to develop.

But there's something else, just as important, which relates to both singles and couples alike: being with someone who truly understands us will not solve all of life's problems. Our society celebrates love to such a degree that we have simply come to expect too much from it. "All You Need Is Love" is a great song by a great band (my favorite one, the Beatles), but it's somewhat misleading. As far as Judaism is concerned, love *cannot* conquer all. It cannot substitute for other important values and relationships that also need to exist for a meaningful and happy life. Love alone cannot defeat the existential loneliness of which we have spoken. Having another person who understands us will certainly help, but the only Being that truly knows us, even better than our life partners, is God who created us. Rabbi Soloveitchik thus writes that Adam and Eve together form a "faith community"—they connect with each other, but their bond also allows each of them to connect with something beyond themselves.

No doubt, marriage helps us meet our physical, emotional, and existential needs, but if that is the only or even the main reason we marry then I fear such a marriage will not withstand the test of time. Husband and wife need to be partners in a mission beyond themselves—they need to have a focus on something higher than each other. The Hebrew word for a man, *ish*, and for a woman, *isha*, differ by two letters, namely, the Hebrew letters *yud* and *hey*, letters which combined spell God's name. The Jewish Sages teach that if God is present in a relationship, man and women can coexist in harmony. However, if God and spirituality are absent, if the Hebrew letters *yud* and *hey* are removed, then all that is left are the letters *aleph* and *shin*, which spells *aish*, or fire. The husband-wife relationship is a potentially explosive one, but when there is a focus on something higher, when the couple work to achieve something *beyond* themselves, the parties will be more fulfilled and the relationship will have a greater chance to last.

Relationships with a Cause

This is precisely the kind of relationship we see between the biblical matriarchs and patriarchs. The first Jewish couple, Abraham and Sarah, spend their lives reaching out and engaging others in their belief of ethical monotheism, which they ultimately pass onto their son Isaac. Isaac then marries Rebecca with whom he partners to spread the Jewish faith. Isaac's view of his marriage to Rebecca as a partnership for a higher mission is hinted at in the biblical verse: *And Isaac brought Rebecca into the tent of Sarah his mother and she became his wife, and he loved her, and Isaac was comforted after the death of his mother.*[13]

A few questions on this verse come to mind: First, why does Isaac bring his new wife Rebecca into his mother Sarah's tent? Sarah had passed away years before and it is therefore odd Isaac would choose to move into the very same home in which his mother had lived. Second, the verse clearly states that it was only *after* Isaac and Rebecca married that Isaac loved her. Did they not love each other before they got married? Finally, the verse concludes by saying that after they married *Isaac was comforted after the death of his mother.* Did it really take all those years for Isaac to be comforted from his mother Sarah's passing?

In answering these questions, Rashi, the French commentator on the Bible, quotes a Jewish tradition from the Midrash: "After Isaac brought Rebecca into his mother's tent she became an image of Sarah, for as long as Sarah was alive the Shabbat candles were lit all week long, there was a special blessing in the dough and God's cloud of glory hovered over the tent."[14] The Midrash continues to say that when Sarah died these three spiritual elements (Shabbat candles, blessing in the dough, and God's cloud of glory) ceased to exist, but when Rebecca entered the tent, they all reappeared. Miraculously, the candles were again lit from week to week, the special blessing in the dough returned, and God's cloud of glory re-appeared, all after Isaac brought Rebecca into his mother's tent.

It appears that Isaac brought Rebecca into his mother Sarah's tent to recreate a home where God's spiritual presence could be felt, like he experienced growing up in his parent's home, which was symbolized by the candles, the dough, and the cloud of glory. That is also why it was only *after* Isaac was married that he felt love for Rebecca because it was only after they created a home together, *after they built something beyond themselves*, that true love developed. That also explains why it is only then that Isaac was finally comforted after the death of his mother. For when Isaac saw that Rebecca had the spiritual power to bring those blessings back into his home, he was reassured he now had a suitable partner with whom he could continue the mission his parents began: to teach the world about a transcendental God and ethical monotheism.

Ultimately Isaac felt love for Rebecca, but only *after* they began to work together as a couple for a higher purpose. Their love was not solely based on what one did for the other, but on what they could accomplish together, as a team, for the rest of the world.

I often wonder whether our marriages today carry a higher purpose beyond the satisfaction of our own needs. I'm not saying couples need to travel to a third world country and feed the poor (although that would certainly be noble). But to ensure the success of our marriages, the relationship needs to contain some selfless giving on behalf of others. One simple example I routinely suggest to newlyweds is setting up other singles, since young couples are often the best networked to make this happen. Another example is hosting people at Shabbat meals, volunteering for a soup kitchen or home for the elderly, or helping any one of many vital causes by raising money or giving one's time.

Please do not misunderstand: Judaism promotes marriage to first and foremost fulfill our legitimate emotional, psychological, and physical needs, and to combat our existential state of loneliness. But is that all? Does the most hallowed institution in Jewish life exist only to satisfy our personal needs? There must be something more.

Ironically, just like with happiness, relationships become stronger when the focus shifts from the couple to helping others. Therefore, when dating, asking yourself questions like "Am I attracted to this person?" or "Are our personalities and interests aligned?" is certainly appropriate, but also make sure to ask yourself "Is this someone with whom I will enjoy helping others?" or "Is this someone with whom I can build a home and raise a family?" That's why dating people who have a similar background or life mission is not being too picky or limiting. If we want our relationships and our marriages to benefit others we need to be with someone who shares this giving outlook. As one of my teachers, Rabbi Aharon Bina, always likes to say, "We don't live for ourselves." Our purpose in this world is to help others and be a light unto the world.

Look for a *giving* nature in others. When Abraham's trusted servant, Eliezer, was sent to find his son (Isaac) a suitable mate, he looked for someone who was kind and who possessed a giving nature. The Bible describes Eliezer, after a very long journey in the hot desert, arriving at a well with his many camels. He tells God he will take it as a divine sign that he has found the right partner for Isaac if one of the young maidens would offer him, a total stranger, and his camels some water. Sure enough, Rebecca steps forward and offers Eliezer water for both him and his camels, and Eliezer invites her to meet Isaac.[15] Eliezer's criterion for a mate was kindness, an indispensable quality for marriage which requires unconditional giving to one's partner. Just as important, though, is the capacity for the couple to give to those outside their marriage.

Numerous highly-respected studies have confirmed links between altruism/giving and stronger marriages.[16] Altruistic love is associated with greater happiness, in general, and particularly more marital happiness, according to a 2006 scientific survey conducted by the National Opinion Research Center at the University of Chicago and supported by the National Science Center. "In the nation's first survey of altruistic love, scholars have found that people who have strong feelings of love for people in general are more likely to have strong romantic relationships [such as marriage]," the release for the survey stated.[17] In a twenty-six-year study of sixty thousand Germans' psychosocial views, researchers found that individuals involved in religion and volunteering enjoyed higher levels of happiness. Married couples who place a priority on altruistic goals say they are happier than people who place a greater priority on career and material success. "The evidence indicates that people who consistently prioritize non-zero sum altruistic goals or family goals are more satisfied with life than people who prioritize goals relating to their own career and material success. Giving priority to altruistic goals is strongly associated with happier life satisfaction," the report said.[18]

As we discussed in chapter one, long-term happiness can only come from giving and working for something greater than oneself. Being faithful, sensitive, and communicative is vital for a healthy marriage, but just as important is being able to work together on behalf of others. Doing so over the course of a lifetime produces true contentment. Marriage is happiness in slow motion. It is a world far *beyond the instant.*

Being a good listener and showing empathy to one's partner is vital, but so is having goals and ideals beyond one's self, and even one's family. That it is why *hachnassat orchim*, or hospitality to strangers, is considered a mitzvah and a core Jewish value in a Jewish home. Inviting guests on a regular basis is not simply a matter of social etiquette, but a way to extend a helping hand to those less fortunate and a means through which one can share the beauty and sanctity of the Sabbath with those with less of a Jewish connection. The Bible describes how Abraham sat at the entrance of his tent so he could invite those passing by to his home for a meal.

A "Jewish home" is not simply a place where Jewish people happen to live, but a place where kindness is extended to all people and where spiritual practices are cultivated—where the spirit of the Sabbath can be felt, the Jewish dietary laws are observed, and the married couple practices the Jewish traditions of sexual intimacy. These three pillars of the Jewish home help the couple weave spiritualty into their everyday lives and into their relationship. These spiritual practices strengthen the relationship precisely because they come from a higher place and are not simply activities one person does for the other. Rather, by observing them the couple builds something *beyond themselves*, which will be immensely beneficial for their children as well.

It is not a surprise that the rates of divorce amongst Jewish couples who practice these traditions are significantly lower than those who do not. A marriage satisfaction survey conducted in 2009 by the Orthodox Union (an organization which supports a large network of synagogues and Jewish youth programs, and provides Kosher certification for food products) of 5,200 Orthodox Jews reported that 72 percent of the men and 74 percent of women rated their marriages as "excellent or very good"[19] compared to a similar survey conducted in the same year by the National Opinion Research Center of the University of Chicago, which reported 63 percent of men and 60 percent of women said they were "very happy" with their marriages.[20]

These findings are consistent with research that indicates that couples who participate in religious activities report greater marital satisfaction and are less likely to divorce than their less observant peers.[21] Religious traditions and lifestyles, coupled with a positive religious education for children, strengthen the family unit by providing the kind of meaning and purpose love alone cannot create.

Thus, for the married folks reading this, the next time you have an opportunity to spend quality time with your husband, wife, or children, consider doing something for someone else. Anytime my family has chosen a giving activity over a taking one, like volunteering at a soup kitchen over going to the movies, it's always brought us closer as a family. In addition, try as much as possible to cultivate the spiritual practices which make up the three pillars of the Jewish home: *Shabbat* (Sabbath), *Kashrut* (dietary laws), and *Tahart Hamishpacha* (Family Purity). They will add a dimension to your life like nothing else can. You have only to gain as individuals and as a family.

If you are single, the next time someone offers to fix you up or the next time you go out on a date, don't just check out the other person's looks, job status, or even their level of sensitivity and kindness. These are all important qualities, of course, but make sure you also explore whether this is someone with whom you can partner to do great things for other people and with whom you can work to build a *giving* home. If all the other qualities you're looking for, be they attraction or compatibility, do not measure up a hundred percent, but they have that partnership quality, think twice before breaking it off. That just may be your soul mate with exactly what you need.

Notes

1. Alex Williams, "Casual Relationships, Yes. Casual Sex, Not Really." *The New York Times*, April 3, 2005. http://www.nytimes.com/2005/04/03/fashion/casual-relationships-yes-casual-sex-not-really.html.
2. Joseph B. Soloveitchik, *The Lonely Man of Faith* (New York: Doubleday, 1965); first appeared in the summer 1965 issue of *Tradition*.

3. Genesis 1:27.
4. Genesis 1:28.
5. Joseph B. Soloveitchik and Abraham R. Besdin, *Man of Faith in the Modern World: Reflections of the Rav,* Volume Two (Hoboken, NJ: Ttav Publishing House, 1989), 47.
6. Ibid, 46.
7. Genesis 2:18.
8. Joseph B. Soloveitchik, *Family Redeemed* (Hoboken, NJ: Ktav Publishing House, Inc., 2000), 16, n20.
9. Ibid, n3.
10. Genesis 4:1.
11. Talmud, Brachot 24a.
12. Genesis 2:24.
13. Genesis 24:67.
14. Rashi on Genesis 24:67.
15. Genesis 24:13–25
16. Amanda Macmillan, "Random Acts of Kindness Make Marriages Happier," *Time* magazine, July 25, 2017, http://time.com/4674982/kindness-compassion-marriage/.
17. The University of Chicago News Office, "Survey links altruism and romantic love," February 9, 2006. http://www-news.uchicago.edu/releases/06/060209.altruism.shtml.
18. Bruce Headey, Ruud Muffels, and Gert G. Wagner, "Long-running German panel survey shows that personal and economic choices, not just genes, matter for happiness," *Proceedings of the National Academy of Sciences of the United States of America,* October 19, 2010, https://www.ncbi.nlm.nih.gov/pmc/articles/PMC2964245/.
19. Orthodox Union Staff, "In National Survey, OU Finds That Orthodox Jewish Marriages Are Stronger than Society as a Whole," January 13, 2010, https://www.ou.org/news/in_national_survey_ou_finds_that_orthodox_jewish_marriages_are_stronger_tha/.
20. Tamar Snyder, "Despite Much to Kvetch About, They're Happy," *Wall Street Journal,* February 19, 2010, https://www.wsj.com/articles/SB10001424052748703525704575061442303169342.
21. Kristen Taylor Curtis and Christopher G. Ellison, "Religious Heterogamy and Marital Conflict Findings of the National Survey of a Family Households," *Journal of Family Issues,* May 1, 2002, http://journals.sagepub.com/doi/abs/10.1177/0192513X02023004005.

Chapter 3
THE POWER OF SEX

Third Commandment: *Thou Shalt Sanctify*

A number of years ago, I was watching TV with my nine-year-old son and a commercial advertising a sleek sports car came on the screen. An attractive and scantily clad woman strutted around the car in a provocative manner. My son, who was very into cars at the time, began to point out some of the unique features of this very cool sports car, but was annoyed by the woman who was getting in the way of the parts of the car he was trying to see. Somewhat agitated he yelled out, "She's blocking my view!" My clearly pre-pubescent son turned to me and asked, "Why is there a woman in this commercial anyway? Aren't they just trying to sell a car?"

Trying to be sensitive but honest, I explained how the advertisers were trying to create an association between owning such a car and attracting a beautiful woman. He was clearly confused, but learned for the first time how broadly and generally sex is used in our world.

What is the ultimate purpose of sexuality? Why are we so drawn to it for physical pleasure and dependent upon it for the perpetuation of our species? And given the way sexuality has become so pervasive in all areas of our lives, how should we approach this sensitive area so we can derive what it was ultimately intended to provide us?

In a wonderful book called *The Hedge of Roses*, Rabbi Dr. Norman Lamm presents the uniquely Jewish approach to sexuality. He first describes the two contradictory concepts of sex which Western-minded people confront, both of which he believes are simply restatements of an ancient attitude toward sex.

One attitude to sex is total openness—the idea that we should embrace anything and everything within the realm of sexuality since ultimately sex is just a natural biological urge, no different than any other bodily function. This view, inspired by Freud and others, looks at the mystery of sex as "romantic nonsense" and condemns traditional religious and moral standards on sexuality as prudery and guilt breeding. Dr. Lamm writes that this permissive view of sex is nothing new: "The psychological veneer and the existentialist vernacular may indeed be novel" but the underlying theories are "those of the paganism that expressed itself in a variety of ways from the sacred prostitution of Canaan to the ribald debauchery of Rome."[1] The "primal urge" and "sanctity of pleasure" were well known in the ancient world and this "new morality," says Dr. Lamm, "is just the old hedonistic immorality in a new and appealing guise."[2]

That is one concept of sexual behavior in our society today. The other view of sex is the exact opposite. As Dr. Lamm puts it, this view of sex "is a puritanical, ascetic, sex negating outlook that is as real as it is denied."[3] This perspective has its source in early Christianity, which taught that sex was the original sin and procreation is what transmits that sin from one generation to another. Paul of Tarsus recommended celibacy, considering marriage as a concession to man's weakness. "Better to marry than to burn with passion," teaches the New Testament.[4] The ideal in Catholicism is not just to control the sexual urge but, if possible, to repress it completely. Christianity continues to struggle with a negative attitude to sex, which Dr. Lamm writes was "born of the disgust with the permissiveness and sex glorification of the ancient pagan world."[5]

Although on the surface it appears we have no allegiance to this perception of sex, Dr. Lamm suggests that deep down this negative perception of sex still strikes deep into our psyche. Since early Christianity and the rise of the Catholic Church as a medieval power influenced the formation of social mores in Western Europe, and to some extent Eastern Europe, the "dirty" view of sex leads a "subterranean life all its own despite our overt contradiction of its claims and principles."[6] Most of us will recognize the presence of this notion of sex as bad: "something which belongs in the gutter but is, by a kind of official hypocrisy, legitimized in the marital chamber."[7]

Simply put, sex is either all good or all bad.

Sex as a Value

Judaism denies both extremes: "[Judaism] rejects paganism's fulsome espousal of uninhibited sexual expression and denies with equal vehemence Christianity's begrudging concept of marriage and its condemnation of all sexual activity as inherently sinful."[8] Depending on how it is approached, classical Judaism looks upon sexuality in a very positive light. A number of Jewish sources lead to this conclusion: The Kabbalah, the Jewish mystical tradition, teaches: "the Shechinah (God's presence) dwells in a home only when a man is married and he cohabits with his wife."[9]

The command of procreation, to be fruitful and multiply, was the very first mitzvah given to humankind. Sex is the means through which God's world is populated and God's will is ultimately carried out. The Jewish Sages therefore saw sex as a "sacred instrument."[10] Even beyond procreation, though, sex in Judaism is viewed as a positive value in and of itself. This is seen in the Torah when man is created and is told by God: "Be fruitful and multiply and fill the earth and subdue her."[11] That phrase, says Dr. Lamm, refers to man's instinctive urge for sex and power. But in the more detailed account of man's creation, where man's moral nature is described, there is no mention of procreation: "And the Lord

God said, it is not good that man should be alone. I will make a help-mate for him . . . Therefore shall a man leave his father and his mother and cleave to his wife and they shall become one flesh."[12] Here, says Dr. Lamm, the loving companionship of husband and wife is an end in itself, separate and apart from procreation.

Another Jewish source which shows that sex has real value beyond having children is found in the *Ketubah*, the Jewish marriage contract. The Ketubah lists the husband's responsibilities toward his wife and includes the husband's obligation to provide his wife with food, clothing, and "satisfaction," referring specifically to the sexual satisfaction the husband is supposed to provide his wife, separate from the Torah's obligation to "be fruitful and multiply"—to have children.

Jewish tradition also teaches that when sex between husband and wife cannot lead to childbearing, for example, while a woman is pregnant or after menopause, sex is still encouraged between husband and wife.

Simply put, Judaism does not see sex as wrong, as a concession to human weakness or as something undesirable but necessary to have children. Sex is ultimately a way for married couples to achieve holiness, depending, of course, on how it is approached. If sanctified, sex can result in much more than physical pleasure, leaving a couple in a state of spiritual holiness.

This explains why the great Jewish philosopher Maimonides, when codifying Jewish law, placed the Jewish laws on Sexuality and *Kashrut* (dietary laws) in the section he called "The Book of Holiness." Interestingly, Maimonides did not include the laws of Yom Kippur or the laws of Prayer in that section, areas we would normally consider "holy," but he did so for sexual conduct and for food consumption. It seems odd to refer to having sex or eating food as something holy, but in Jewish thought that is precisely the goal of these activities.

Holiness, according to many great rabbis, is defined as the ability to elevate oneself above the physical so one can direct their physical activities toward something higher than simply the personal pleasure they produce. Maimonides chose to place the laws of sexuality and *kashrut* in the

Book of Holiness because it is precisely in these very physical areas of sex and eating, activities we share with the animal world, that we are challenged to direct them toward a higher goal. In doing so we become holy. It may seem more appropriate to be "holy" in a synagogue or in a house of study, but Judaism's aim is to live a *life* of holiness. Life happens, not in study halls or synagogues, but in our bedrooms and kitchens.

Sex and Food

How can sex or eating be elevated to become a holy experience?

In the case of food, applying the Torah's laws of *kashrut* helps develop us into more disciplined people by ensuring that our food choices are not solely based on what looks good on a menu, but upon the wishes of one's Creator expressed in the Torah and practiced by Jews throughout the millennia.

Eating is used not simply to survive, but to become a more disciplined and spiritual person. The more mystically inclined rabbis teach that refraining from non-Kosher food enables the body to become a more accepting vessel for spirituality and divine closeness. The Kabbalah relates that certain foods, non-Kosher ones specifically, make it more difficult for the body to carry out the aims of the soul. Since most non-Kosher animals are carnivorous by nature, the concern is that by eating those animals, we will somehow internalize their cruel habits. As the saying goes, "you are what you eat." Either way, approaching the whole eating experience from a Torah perspective elevates the person who eats to a higher spiritual state compared to one who eats simply to survive or just to enjoy the food.

The same goes for sex, which also can be approached as a purely biological activity. However, if sex is used to express love between two people within the committed framework of marriage, it is an important vehicle in creating a state of holiness and sanctity between the couple. As discussed in chapter two, giving creates love and the giving of physical pleasure involved in sex helps develop the love and strengthen the commitment and trust of a couple, and builds more of a solid foundation for the home they together create. This is precisely why Judaism views sex not as a *prerequisite* for a relationship, but as an indispensable means for an already committed couple to deepen their commitment.

The sexual union also creates the kind of intimacy necessary to achieve the level of oneness the Torah wishes the couple to reach: *"Therefore should man leave his father and mother and cleave unto his wife and they will be one flesh."*[13] As discussed in chapter two, one of the goals of marriage is for the couple to be as one, feeling the joy and pain of their partner as though it was their own. Sex is necessary to make that happen.

The spiritual and emotional value of sex can also be seen in the Jewish laws governing sexual intimacy between husband and wife, what the Jewish Sages call *Taharat Hamishpacha*, or Family Purity. This religious practice calls for a period of sexual abstention each month beginning with the onset of the woman's menstrual cycle. This period of separation not only helps create a healthy sexual longing between the couple, but ensures that each month the couple also relates to one another in a non-physical way. That forces the couple to deal with their relationship issues and not simply settle them in bed. Successful marriages tend to yield this kind of conversation, but the traditions of Family Purity provide a real path toward this goal.

Learning to be intimate without being physical is critical, since intimacy requires a deep emotional connection that Judaism believes should be expressed physically through sex, but not be based on it. Relationships need a foundation that is deeper than the physical. Observing this period of abstention helps maintain that balance, and ensures that the couple's sexual union remains part of something deeper and more long-lasting than the few moments of physical gratification it may produce. It's learning to live *beyond the instant*.

Please do not misunderstand: within the context of marriage where the couple is committed to one another and to building something beyond themselves, there's nothing wrong with approaching sex for its pure physical pleasure. Judaism, after all, is not an ascetic religion and as such does not believe in denying oneself the physical pleasures of the world. In fact, the Talmud says that God calls one to task for not enjoying the permitted pleasures of this world.[14] Judaism therefore never asks us to completely deny physical pleasures, but rather restricts them to some degree to ensure that we not only derive physical pleasure from God's world, but also the deeper and more lasting spiritual meaning.

The Benefits of Limitations

Thus, when it comes to sex or really any physical pleasure, ultimately, it is left in our hands to do as we please. We can sanctify the sexual or eating experiences or any part of our physical lives with the goal of attaining something deeper, or we can approach those same activities with the simple goal of achieving physical pleasure. But because the pleasure is so short-lived, because it's over so quickly, we're on to the next pleasure before we even know it. I always feel this after a long fast day when all I can think about in those last few hours of the fast is a bagel and a nice hot cup of coffee. Then I break the fast, and literally within minutes that awesome feeling of eating I've been thinking about all day is gone! The quick high we get from sex or food, when not coupled with something deeper, ends up being more of a tease than anything else. They provide some pleasure but they don't fill us with any real long-lasting sense of gratification.

In fact, the pleasure reduces. As both the Sages teach and modern studies confirm, there's a diminishing return when it comes to physical pleasure. At a certain point, the more we engage in sex or the more food we eat, the *less* physical gratification we derive from the experience. Rabbi Yochanan, a Sage of the Talmud, taught: "There is a small organ in man; when he starves it he is sated, and when he satiates it he is hungry."[15] According to a major study published in the journal *Social Psychology and Personality Science* in 2015 and conducted by researchers at the University of Toronto, there's an upper limit to improving well-being among couples through sex of about once a week. The data "showed a linear association between sex and happiness up to a frequency of once a week, but at higher frequencies there is no longer an association," said Amy Muise, a social psychologist at the University of Toronto, who led the research. "Therefore it is not necessary, on average, for couples to aim to engage in sex as frequently as possible."[16]

I am not sharing this information to discourage married couples from having sex more than once a week (there is no such Jewish tradition), but to demonstrate the Torah's wisdom behind the restrictions Judaism does have regarding sexual intimacy. Sometimes less is more and I believe the Torah restricts a married couples' physical intimacy during the woman's menstrual cycle and shortly thereafter, not to simply limit their pleasure, but to ensure the couple *continues* to derive pleasure and that they are left with something lasting and real, *beyond the instant*.

In the case of food, the *kashrut* restrictions help build discipline and a more receptive body to receive spiritual enlightenment. When it comes to sex, the restrictions help the couple approach their physical relationship in a way, not only to derive physical pleasure, but to build intimacy and a stronger relationship by conditioning the couple to use sex as a method of giving. The giving builds the couple's love, one of the truly non-physical parts of life that will always continue to grow. Unlike sex there is no diminishing point of return for love. The more you feed it, the more it grows. The love then becomes the basis for the creation of the home, from which children are developed and nurtured, and a place where outsiders can also be helped and supported.

Sex is the fuel for all this. Or it can just be sex. The choice is ours.

The Prostitute and Religious Student

This profound choice, with which we are all confronted when it comes to sexuality, is powerfully taught by a fascinating story in the Talmud:

> There was a man extremely careful in the observance of the commandment of Tzizit, the wearing of ritual fringes on the

four corners of one's garment. Once he heard that there was a prostitute in a city by the sea whose fee was four hundred gold pieces. He sent her the four hundred gold pieces and a time was arranged for him. When the day arrived, he went to the door of her house. Her maid went in and told her: 'That man who sent you the four hundred pieces of gold has come and sits at the door.' Said she: 'Let him enter.' He entered. She had prepared for him seven beds, six of silver and one of gold. They were arranged one above the other and between each there was a ladder made of silver. The highest bed was the one of gold. She climbed up to the top and lay down naked in the golden bed. Then he too climbed up to sit down opposite her in the nude. At this moment, the four fringes of his garb came and slapped him across the face. At this moment, he broke away and sat down on the ground. She too came down and sat on the ground. Said she to him: 'By the Capitol of Rome! I shall not let you off until you tell me what blemish you saw in me.' Said he to her: 'I swear I have never seen a woman as beautiful as you, but there is a commandment that God commanded us, its name is Tzizit. The words in which they are written contain the phrase, I am the Lord your God twice, meaning: I am the one who calls to account; I am the one who will reward. Now, they (i.e.—the Tzizit) appeared to me as if they were four witnesses.' Said she to him: 'I shall not let you off till you tell me your name, the name of your city, of your rabbi, the name of the school where you study Torah.' He wrote it all down and placed it in her hand. Then she got up and divided all her property into three parts: a third for the government, a third for the poor, and a third she took with her, apart from that bed linen (which was not included in the division). She proceeded to the study house of Rabbi Hiyya and said to him: 'Rabbi! Command that I be made a convert.' Said he to her: 'My daughter, is it perhaps that one of the students appealed to your eyes?' She took the note (that he had given to her) from her hand

and gave it to him. Whereupon (after reading it) he said to her: 'Go and take possession of what you have acquired.' The story concludes with this moral: "And so the same bed linen that she once spread out for him to serve his lust, she now spread out for him in consecrated union.[17]

The same activity, between the same two people, could be viewed as sinful or sanctified. It all depends on the context—whether the sexuality was used to simply satisfy the physical desires of a young man, or also as an expression of love between two people in a committed relationship. And it all becomes symbolized in the bed linen: the same object that was used to satisfy the young man's lust was ultimately used in "consecrated union." The couple in the story had obviously married and in the context of that kind of committed relationship sexuality becomes holy, a consecrated union.

The symbolism of a prostitute is also very telling. The biblical term for a prostitute is *kedaysha*, taken from the word *kadosh* or holy. Sex has within it the potential for true holiness—it just depends on how we approach it and ultimately how we use it. It can be a *kadosh* experience when it expresses love and commitment but it can also be *kedaysha*, "prostituted," when used only to serve our base physical desires. It all depends on what we do with it.

In a day and age where sex is used for so many other things—to sell products, to make money—for so many purposes *other* than to express love and commitment, the Torah challenges us to use this gift for the greatest possible purpose: to give and to build something greater than ourselves, and in doing so sanctify and make us holy people.

Notes

1. Rabbi Dr. Norman Lamm, *A Hedge of Roses* (New York: Feldheim Publishers, 1987), 20.
2. Ibid, 21.
3. Ibid, 22.

4. 1 Corinthians 7:9.
5. Lamm, *A Hedge of Roses*, 23.
6. Ibid.
7. Ibid, 24.
8. Ibid.
9. Zohar 1:122a.
10. Lamm, *A Hedge of Roses*, 26.
11. Genesis 1:26.
12. Genesis 2:18–25.
13. Genesis 2:24.
14. Jerusalem Talmud, Kiddushin 4:12.
15. Talmud, Succah 52b.
16. Nancy Shute, "Is Sex Once a Week Enough for a Happy Relationship?" NPR, November 18, 2015, https://www.npr.org/sections/health-shots/2015/11/18/456482701/is-sex-once-a-week-enough-for-a-happy-relationship.
17. Talmud, Menachot 44a.

Chapter 4

ACHIEVING SUCCESS

Fourth Commandment: *Thou Shalt Fail*

I come from a big family of lawyers. My father has been practicing immigration law for decades, representing high-profile clients like John Lennon and other musicians and artists. My brother began his legal career as a federal prosecutor and is now in private practice, representing some pretty big celebrities as well. My sister-in-law is a lawyer. My cousins are all successful attorneys. Then it was my turn. I went to law school, and after I graduated I set out to study for the bar. I'll never forget the day the results from the Bar Exam came in the mail. I was so excited. I had waited for this moment for a long time. I opened the letter and to my utter dismay, I'd failed! I couldn't believe it. I had this terrible pit in the bottom of my stomach. I was so disappointed and embarrassed, but I wasn't deterred. I signed up for a different bar review course and I studied again. I took the exam a second time and . . . I failed, again. I was totally humiliated—a Wildes failing the bar twice! I didn't want anyone to know I had failed, and there was no way I was going to take that test again.

Studies from the 1960s to the present demonstrate how fear of failure prevents people of all ages from achieving some of their most important dreams and goals in life. I see this every day in my work with young men and women—how fear of failure prevents people from going on a diet, tackling a new project at work, or pursuing an important relationship. Fear of failure is affecting younger people today more than ever. For people entering the workforce in recent years, the financial crash of 2008 and years of economic anxiety have spurred an increase in the fear of failure. While entrepreneurship has increased since the crash, millennials are not leading the way. Data studied by the US Small Business Administration shows that among all entrepreneurs, millennials are starting fewer businesses per capita than older generations. The *Wall Street Journal* reported on a study which concluded that startup companies initiated by people in their twenties are at their lowest point in the last twenty-four years, down from 10.3 percent in 1989 to 3.8 percent in 2013.[1]

This means that the population most suited to risk taking, young healthy twentysomethings who are unaccountable to spouses, children, or mortgages, are today the smallest group of risk takers. The largest growing group of entrepreneurs in the United States today are ages fifty and up!

Overcoming a fear of failure isn't just an economic issue. It's about the best of the human spirit and our relationship with God. I have been privileged to witness people overcome failure and adversity with great persistence, but none greater than my lifelong friend David Keen.

After high school, like most of our friends David and I went off to study in Israel for our gap year before starting college. Over the course of the year abroad David started experiencing problems with his eyesight. At first, he had a difficult time reading the smaller, finer commentaries of the Talmud, then he was having trouble reading the text itself. By the end of the year David had gone almost completely blind. We came back to New York and went to college together; to be honest I wondered how he'd ever make it through class, take tests, date girls, and have a normal life.

Fast-forward, David not only finished college, but he was accepted to rabbinical school and together we became rabbis. I used to see him sitting in the study hall until one or two in the morning listening to audio-tapes of the rabbinical classes. He must have listened to hundreds of class tapes and taken dozens of oral exams to make it through college and rabbinical school; he even completed a master's degree in Social Work. David met a great woman, got married, and began to raise children.

But there were many times throughout those years when things were not working out for David. His studies and social life were moving very slowly; he felt like he was failing and just wanted to quit. Simple tasks he used to take for granted became huge chores. But David never gave up. He just kept plugging away. Occasionally I'd bring a friend into the Jewish study hall late at night just so they could see David sitting there listening to one of the hundreds of tapes he had to master to become a rabbi. The sight of David working so hard, trying to overcome his many obstacles, became inspiring to us, his many friends.

Today, David has a beautiful family and serves as a chaplain in the New York City hospital system, giving aid and encouragement to patients. He had so many justifications along the way to give up, to succumb to the failure he was already experiencing, but he just kept going until he got it right. I see David often as our children are now in school together, and I often imagine how different his life would be today, *had he* given up.

Rabbi Yitzchak Hutner, one of the great rabbinic scholars of the twentieth century, taught that growth comes from struggle and that we become bigger when we fall. The Talmud records that only four people died without ever sinning. However, even those well acquainted with Jewish tradition are generally unaware of who those people are. They never became well-known because they were never considered *tzadikim*, the Jewish term for a righteous person. This is because the test of a *tzadik*, the measure of a righteous individual, is how he or she overcomes adversity, and how they rise from the ashes.

But it's easier said than done. The average person seems incapable of such perseverance. Getting up after failing is an enormous challenge with which most of us struggle.

Failure as a Prerequisite for Success

What is Judaism's recipe for persevering in the face of challenge and failure? Remembering that failure is something we must go through so we can eventually succeed.

One of the very first verses in the Bible reads: "And there was evening and there was morning, day one."[2] The Jewish Sages ask a simple question: Why does the verse read "and there was evening?" The word *and* implies there was something beforehand, yet this was the very first day of creation! What existed before the world was created?

The Sages answer that there were many worlds created before this one: "Rabbi Abbahu said: This proves that the Holy One, blessed be He, went on creating worlds and destroying them until He created this one and declared, 'This one pleases Me; those do not please Me.'"[3] The Midrash suggests that the world in which we live was not the first one God willed into existence. Rather, the Almighty created *many* worlds, hundreds, before He created the one in which we live today.

Why would a perfect God need to create hundreds of worlds before creating the final one? Could the Almighty not get it right the first time?

As my mentor and teacher, one of the foremost scholars of our time, Rabbi Dr. Jacob J. Schacter, remarked, this Jewish teaching says nothing about God, but everything about us. God is teaching us that we may have to try something many times before we get it right. By creating and destroying until the desired end is achieved, we are taught not to give up when something does not come out the way we wanted the first, second, or even the hundredth time. The great inventor, Thomas Edison, went through over nine thousand experiments in trying to develop the alkaline storage battery. When his friend and associate Walter Mallory learned that not one of those experiments produced any positive results, he asked Edison: "Isn't it a shame that with the tremendous amount of work you have done you haven't been able to get any results?" To which Edison, with a smile, responded: "Results!

Why, man, I have gotten lots of results! I [now] know several thousand things that won't work!"[4]

Failure is a necessary step in achieving success.

Abraham Lincoln is another extraordinary person who rebounded from difficult, wrenching setbacks. In many ways, the trials of his life prepared him for winning the grim cataclysm of the US Civil War. At the age of nine, Lincoln's mother died, a special hardship for a struggling farm family. Lincoln later lost his modest job in 1831, and in 1833, tried another business which failed. He was defeated for the State Legislature in 1832. His fiancée died in 1835, and, in 1836, he suffered a nervous breakdown. In 1843, Lincoln failed to achieve his party's nomination, and in 1849, he sought the federal position of Land Officer, but lost. Lincoln withdrew from the Senate race in 1855 because he didn't have the requisite majority votes, and, in 1858 he failed to win a seat in the Senate. Finally, in 1860, Abraham Lincoln was elected the sixteenth president of the United States.

Persistence despite failure is the only way to eventually attain success. The great Chasidic master, Reb Levi of Berdichev, taught that one of the things an adult can learn from a baby is that no matter how many times a baby falls, it always gets up. Somehow the baby naturally intuits that to eventually walk it needs to keep getting up every time it falls. Falling or failing is the way we humans learn to grow and develop. That is, if we learn from our mistakes! The greatest college basketball coach of all time, John Wooden (his team won the NCAA championship eleven times in thirteen years), would always say: "Failure isn't fatal, but failure to change might be."

Failing versus *Being* a Failure

But if this is all true, if failing and learning from our failures is something we all must go through to eventually succeed, and if so many great people we admire failed, then why does it make us feel so bad about ourselves? In my own personal situation, why did I have that terrible pit in my stomach when I learned I had failed the bar exam? Why are we so embarrassed by our failures?

To answer this question, we need to go back to the very beginning of creation. You may be familiar with the following story in the Bible: Adam and Eve are placed in the Garden of Eden and told by God they can enjoy the fruit from any of the beautiful trees in this paradise, except for the tree of knowledge. The serpent entices Eve, who in turn convinces Adam, and they eat from the forbidden fruit. Adam and Eve sin. According to Christianity, that "original sin" so tainted Adam and Eve's souls that it contaminated all of humankind and rendered all people incapable of achieving goodness on their own. To be redeemed, humanity must place its faith in someone untainted by original sin, since mankind is incapable of saving itself.[5]

In Judaism, original sin plays an important role, albeit a very different one. The Kabbalists (Jewish mystical thinkers) teach that before Adam and Eve sinned, they existed on a very high spiritual plain, almost like angels, possessing only a *yetzer tov*, a good inclination. There was evil in the world, but it was external to man and woman. When they sinned, they brought that negativity within themselves and from that point on mankind would possess not only the *yetzer tov*, the inclination toward the good and positive, but also a *yetzer hara*, a negative inclination. These two opposing forces would now have to battle it out for control, but according to Judaism, the *yetzer tov* can prevail over the *yetzer hara*. Through the exercise of free will, the good within us can prevail over the bad, and in doing so humankind can save themselves.

Rabbi Meir Soloveitchick, a popular rabbi, scholar, and expert on comparative religion, asserts that this difference in outlook, between believing that one needs a savior versus being able to save oneself, explains *who the Messiah is* in each of these traditions: In Christianity, the Messiah is someone born as the product of a virgin birth and a Divine father. The Catholic Church asserted the well-known doctrine of *immaculate conception*, which posits that even Jesus's mother Mary was somehow untainted by Adam's original sin and that she existed without urges or desires, tempted by nothing but the opportunity to serve God. She was perfect.

In Jewish tradition, however, the Messiah is a descendant of the biblical figure King David, whose family is far from being perfect. King David comes from the tribe of Judah, a great man who emerges as the leader of all the tribes. However, the Bible also tells us of the incident in which Judah has relations with his own daughter-in law, who, when desperate for a child, dressed up as a prostitute.[6] Peretz, who was born from that union, was conceived out of wedlock. King David's most famous *female* ancestor, Ruth, was a Moabite who converted to Judaism. Moab's lineage was even more questionable than Peretz, tracing its biblical origins to a relationship that wasn't only promiscuous, but incestuous, namely, that of Lot and his daughter. Furthermore, the nation of Moab from whom David's ancestor Ruth came, is described in the Torah as a dangerous enemy of Israel, whose women enticed the Israelites to engage in idol worship, bringing plague and destruction into the Jewish community.

And even after David is designated as King of Israel and the ancestor of the Jewish messiah, he chooses not the progeny of Michal, daughter of King Saul, as his heir to the throne, but rather his son Solomon, son of Bathsheba, whose relationship with David was also tainted by sexual sin. King David was a great prophet and warrior, but as the Bible describes he had enemies and he struggled with his own personal issues, including sin. However, through struggle and hard work David overcame those obstacles by engaging in a process of *teshuva*—of repentance—ultimately returning to the proper spiritual path.

When you understand the *purpose* of the Messiah in each of these traditions, the difference between Jesus and David as messianic models makes perfect sense: in Christianity, the Messiah comes to redeem an impure world incapable of redeeming itself, and so Jesus and his lineage must be perfect. According to Judaism, since humankind can and must save *itself*, David (and his predecessors Judah and Ruth)—a great but imperfect leader who overcomes his own imperfections—inspires the world to earn its own redemption.

To put this in superhero terms, the difference between Jesus and David is the difference between Superman and Batman. Born on another planet, Superman, this picture-perfect specimen with supernatural powers, is sent to earth to save a race incapable of saving itself. Superman is Jesus. Place your faith in someone who is perfect and can save you, because you can't save yourself.

Batman, on the other hand, is more like the Jewish superhero because he has no supernatural powers. He can't fly or burn through steel with his eyes, but he uses his *human* powers to fight crime and make a difference. He uses his intellect, detective skills, science, and technology. Batman isn't from some planet far way, but a rich kid who sees his parents murdered before his eyes. He's faced with the real choice of using his talents and gifts to help society or live the life of a spoiled playboy. He's got a dark side and struggles to turn his childhood trauma involving bats into his greatest strength.

Batman must first battle his inner demons before he can fight the bad guys of Gotham. He must first conquer his *yetzer hara*, the evil inclination within him. Superman does not have to do any of this because Superman is perfect. He has no *yester hara* against which he must battle, but he's also not human. He may dress up like Clark Kent but that's not who is. Batman on the other hand is just Bruce Wayne who dresses up like a superhero. But as far as I'm concerned, he's the real "superman" because he's a mortal being who successfully overcomes his internal struggle and leverages his talents and resources for the good of society. Batman represents the ability we all possess to redeem ourselves and make a positive difference in the world, however flawed we may be. For although we have weaknesses and although we err and sin, we are not fundamentally *sinners*.

We may *fail*, but that doesn't mean we are *failures*.

This is ultimately why I think we feel so awful when we fail. Christianity is a major source of Western thought and I believe that on some level, somewhere in the back of our minds, we've internalized this idea that we're fundamentally flawed and this thought gets triggered when we fail at something important. We imagine at those moments that we haven't simply failed in that endeavor, on that exam, on that diet, or in that relationship, but that fundamentally we're *failures*.

This is *not* a Jewish idea. There is no source anywhere in biblical or Rabbinic literature which supports this concept. In fact, on Yom Kippur, the holiest day of the Jewish calendar, when we ask God for forgiveness, we recite a prayer called the Vidduy (the confessional). The prayer contains a long list of sins we have committed over the past year to which we confess. But nowhere in that prayer do we ever refer to ourselves as *sinners*. We may sin but that doesn't mean we're sinners.

When King David, Moses, and other prophets of the Bible made mistakes or transgressed, they never asked for God's mercy as *sinners*. They came before God honest and humble enough to admit they had done wrong, but still with a basic belief in themselves, precisely the way we all appear before the Almighty on Yom Kippur or anytime we pray: as individuals who have made mistakes but who can do better, *not* as metaphysically flawed beings incapable of repairing the damage we've caused through our sins. At no point do our prayers describe our sins as indicative of a deeper, sinful human state. In fact, one of the prayers Jews traditionally recite each morning starts like this: "My God, the soul you placed within me is pure." Note the grammatical tense: "The soul you placed within me *is* pure." We don't say the soul God gave us *was* pure, when the Almighty first created Adam *before* he sinned. We say the soul given to us *today* is pure. For each of us still has a soul that yearns to be closer to its Divine source, a part of us that wants to do the right thing. We begin our day by stressing the purity and holiness we have within us.

When we sin or fail we may *feel* like sinners or failures, but we are not.

Rabbi Akiva: The Eternal Optimist

An "eternal optimist" is the only way I can explain the extraordinary optimism of my favorite rabbinic figure in the Talmud, Rabbi Akiva.

Perhaps more than any other rabbi of the Talmudic period, Rabbi Akiva is confronted with tremendous difficulties and challenges. Somehow though, he remains the eternal optimist, always brushing off the dust and moving on. The Talmud relates that after overcoming great personal obstacles in becoming a Torah scholar, and then after developing a huge following, Rabbi Akiva suffers the loss of his 24,000 students who all died in a mysterious epidemic.

The reason the Talmud gives for their death makes this episode even more devastating: "for they failed to give proper respect to one another."[7] Rabbi Akiva, whose life mantra was "love your neighbor," must have felt like a complete failure, having lost thousands of his beloved students for failing to properly internalize one of his chief teachings. Besides the enormous human loss, his whole life work was destroyed in a matter of weeks. And yet the Talmud relates that after suffering the loss of his many students, Rabbi Akiva traveled to the south of Israel where he found more students to teach. The Talmud lists their names: *Rebbi Meir, Rebbi Yehuda, Rebbe Yossi, Rebbe Eliezer ben Shamua and Rebbe Shimon bar Yocha.* Rabbi Akiva found these five new students, taught them, and ultimately ordained them, enabling them to become the new scholars of the next generation.

How did Rabbi Akiva do this? How did he not simply remain devastated after his initial efforts proved unsuccessful? I would suggest that Rabbi Akiva, even in the face of tragedy and failure, never branded *himself* a failure. He may have failed with that large group of students, but that didn't mean he was fundamentally flawed and incapable of ever teaching again. Other episodes related in the Talmud about Rabbi Akiva depict him as an incurable optimist, for he still saw in himself and in his people the potential for greatness and was thus able to carry on and continue to teach and inspire.

Believing in Ourselves

This message isn't just pop psychology designed to make you and me feel better the next time we fail. Belief in ourselves is considered a fundamental principle and article of faith in the Jewish religion. The great Maimonides wrote that for the Messiah to come, the Jewish people must become worthy of its arrival by engaging in *teshuva*, by repenting and returning to God's ways as outlined in the Torah.[8] Repentance is a prerequisite for messianic redemption. The same Maimonides wrote elsewhere that it is considered one of the thirteen principles of the Jewish faith to believe in the coming of the Messiah.[9] The twentieth century sage Rabbi Joseph Soloveitchik posed the following question: How could Maimonides say the Messiah will only come if the Jewish people repent and return to the ways of Torah, when Maimonides also maintains that one of the fundamental principles of Judaism is for all Jews to believe in the coming of the Messiah? What if the Jewish people never repent? What if the Jewish people do not return to living a life of Torah and mitzvoth? How then can you believe in the Messianic redemption?

The simple answer is you can't. The only way to believe in the coming of the Messiah, suggests Rabbi Soloveitchick, is to believe in the capacity of the Jewish people to do *teshuva*, to return to living a life of Torah and mitzvoth. Since believing in Messianic redemption is a fundamental principle of Judaism and since that Messiah can only come if the people become *worthy* of its arrival, the belief in the Messiah is ultimately a belief in the Jewish people. It turns out that the principle to believe in the Messiah is really a belief in ourselves. If we can't believe in the capacity of our own people to live lives of purpose and nobility, lives of Torah and mitzvoth, then ultimately, we cannot believe in the coming of the Messiah, a cornerstone of the Jewish faith.

If you doubt this or struggle with this idea, just remember that thousands of years ago God came to our ancestors and revealed to them the Torah, a book of laws which came with hundreds of commandments: the command to love our neighbors as ourselves, to deal kindly with the stranger, to give charity, to observe the Sabbath, to keep kosher and many more. If God didn't think us capable of observing these laws why would he have given us the Torah in the first place? The God of Judaism commands us to observe His laws, not only because He thinks they're the best thing for us, but also because He believes we're capable of living up to them.

In the most important part of the daily prayers, the Silent Devotion, before we ask God for forgiveness for our sins, we acknowledge the wisdom and insight with which we are endowed. We first say, "you have bestowed upon man wisdom," and only after do we ask, "please forgive us our father for we have sinned." As Rabbi Meir Soloveitchik points out, only after we recognize the wisdom and insight we possess, the greatness within us, do we then ask God for forgiveness. I find this prayer inspiring because it reminds us to focus on what we have accomplished and our unique strengths as human beings. If we start with our flaws and mistakes, if we identify more with our limitations, then we stymie the part of us that can do better and which *has* the power to succeed.

I share this message every year with my students on the High Holidays when I ask why so many of us define ourselves as a "two-time-a-year-synagogue Jew" simply because that's the way we were raised. Why are we not trying to identify with a different part of ourselves that wants a deeper spiritual connection, and thus come to pray and study more often? The irony is that in America we pride ourselves on being able to do whatever we choose. We believe we can succeed in ways our parents did not, that the child of a taxi driver can become a real estate mogul or a US Senator. We should apply the same belief in our potential to *every* sphere of our existence, in our spiritual lives and in our relationships as well.

I was facing such a crossroads in my own life back in 1998. I was finishing up my work as assistant rabbi at Kehilath Jeshurun (KJ), a wonderful synagogue on the East Side of Manhattan, and I wasn't sure which way to head. I could stay in the rabbinate or go back into law. I was also very passionate about Jewish outreach, having spent the last seven years involved in Jewish education to the unaffiliated. I went to a dear friend, George Rohr, a venture capitalist, philanthropist, and leader of KJ's outreach activities, for guidance. George said he wanted to think about it. He called me a few days later and said, "Rabbi, I think you should start an outreach program and I'm willing to offer you some seed money to get it started, but on one condition: that this is the *only* thing you do professionally." That made the decision much harder because until that point I'd had my hand in different pots, which I liked, not to mention the fact that I'd somehow have to raise the rest of the money for the first year's budget and every year to come and I'd never raised a penny in my life. I discussed it with my wife, Jill, and she was very excited and supportive (as she continues to be to this day), but I was still nervous. Could I really do this? So I did what I've always done when I need to make an important decision: I went to my father for advice. My father listened attentively and asked, "Mark, what do you really want to do?" "I want to take George up on his offer to start an outreach program," I answered, "but I'm scared; maybe I won't be successful." My father looked at me and said, "Mark, don't be afraid, I know you can do this. Your mother and I always believed in you and if you do this I'll be there every step along the way to help."

And so MJE was born. It started with a father's belief in his son. I remember thinking: if the person I most look up to in life thinks I can do it, then maybe I can.

Imagine if everyone had people like that in their lives—how far each of us could go. It was George's and my father's belief in me that started MJE, and ultimately it is our belief in the capacity of every person that remains the basis for this organization. MJE is premised on the fundamental greatness and potential of every person, no matter their background.

We just need to believe in ourselves as God Himself does.

This is why, in Jewish tradition, we begin our day each morning by thanking God, not only for giving us life, but for believing in us: *I thank you O everlasting King, for returning to me my soul with compassion.* We begin the prayer by thanking God for waking us up, for giving us another day in His beautiful world, but then we end the prayer with four powerful words: *great is your faithfulness.*[10] We don't say great is *our faith in you,* God, but rather, great is the faith *you have in us.* We know the Almighty has this faith in us because after all, He allowed us to wake up—He gave us another day to live, and God must therefore have thought us capable of fulfilling the purpose for our creation.

So the next time you fail, and you will, brush off the dust, pick yourself up, and start over again. Just because you were unsuccessful at something doesn't mean you're a failure. We may fail but we are not failures. We may sin but we are not sinners. We have a *yetzer hara*, we have inner demons, struggles, and obstacles, but we also have been given the Torah as a guide and we have role models like King David and even Batman to inspire us to use our own abilities to overcome those obstacles and become the people we were meant to be.

I took the bar a third time and, thankfully, I finally passed. For to succeed we often need to fail—but that *never* means we're failures.

Notes

1. Ruth Simon and Caelainn Barr, "Endangered Species: Young U.S. Entrepreneurs," *Wall Street Journal*, January 2, 2015, https://www.wsj.com/articles/endangered-species-young-u-s-entrepreneurs-1420246116.
2. Genesis 1:5.
3. Midrash, Bereshit Rabbah 3:7.
4. Frank Dyer and T.C. Martin, *Edison: His Life and Inventions*, CreateSpace Independent Publishing Platform, June 30, 2016.
5. Joint statement issued in 1998 by Evangelicals and Catholics: *God created us to manifest his glory and to give us eternal life in fellowship with himself, but our disobedience intervened and brought us under condemnation. As members of the fallen human race, we come into the world estranged from God and in a state of rebellion. This original sin is compounded by our personal acts of sinfulness. The catastrophic consequences of sin are such that we are powerless to restore the ruptured bonds of union with God. Only in the light of what God has done to restore our fellowship with him do we see the full enormity of our loss. The gravity of our plight and the greatness of God's love are brought home to us by the life, suffering, death, and resurrection of Jesus Christ . . . . The restoration of communion with God is absolutely dependent upon Jesus Christ, true God and true man, for he is "the one mediator between God and men," and "there is no other name under heaven given among men by which we must be saved."* (www.christiantruth.com/articles/ect2.html)
6. Genesis 38.
7. Talmud, Yevamot 62b.
8. Maimonides , Mishna Torah, Laws of Repentance 7:5.
9. Maimonides, Commentary on the Mishna, Sanhedrin Chapter 10.
10. *The Koren Siddur* (Jerusalem: Koren Publishers), 5.

Chapter 5

THE BLAME GAME

Fifth Commandment: *Thou Shalt Take Responsibility*

One of the world's great violinists, Isaac Stern, was once playing a Mozart violin concerto with the New York Philharmonic. Midway through the first movement Isaac Stern experienced a lapse of memory. He literally forgot the music. He stopped playing, walked over to the conductor, and asked if he and the orchestra could start over and begin the concerto again. Stern turned to the very large audience, apologized for his mistake, and began to play the same music all over again.

A critic reviewing the incident said, "A man of his ability could have fooled his audience and covered up his mistakes and yet his faithfulness to Mozart and to his music demanded of him a clear accounting of his error and a desire to start all over again."[1]

That was Isaac Stern, already one of the great classical violinists in history. Meet the girls from the Danville, Vermont, high school basketball team. On January 11, 2002, five members of their team showed up for their big game, but they weren't wearing their uniforms because they weren't permitted to play. Their coach, Tammy Rainville, had a zero-tolerance rule when it came to drugs and alcohol for any members of the team. On New Year's Eve these five girls had gone to a party and drank. When classes resumed after the break and accounts of holiday parties were shared, rumors about the five girls began closing in on them. The girls got together and decided to go to the coach with the full story.

The coach said she couldn't back down on her policy even though four of the five were starters, the best players on the team. The players agreed to come to the game to show their support for the coach's decision. After the team lost the game, one of the girls asked if she could say a few words. With the other four standing beside her, she said to the school: "We hope you will understand that we are not bad kids. We made a mistake . . . what we did was definitely not worth it. We hope this event will make everyone open their eyes and realize that there is a big drug and alcohol problem in our community. If you work with us to try to solve this problem, you will help us feel that we have not been thrown off our basketball team for nothing." The five left the floor to deafening applause, and the Danville High School girls basketball team didn't win any more games that year, but the girls took responsibility for their actions. They didn't point the finger elsewhere or make excuses—"well, everyone at the party was drinking" or "that's what I saw in my home." They owned up to what they had done and as a result were able to grow from the situation themselves and set a rare example for other students facing the same challenge.[2]

Do you take responsibility for your own mistakes? When something goes wrong, do you look at yourself or do you point the finger elsewhere and blame others?

Employers today are expressing concerns about this as a trend. A survey by SmartRecruiter of 28,000 bosses showed their millennial workers were failing to take responsibility in the workplace. Millennials, having been coached their whole lives, expect their employers to provide on-the-job training to complete their job tasks. Employers (especially small to mid-size businesses with limited budgets and resources) felt their millennial employees need to take responsibility for their own training and development via online tools and resources, instead of depending on the company to do so. The survey also found that bosses felt their millennial workers struggled to find happiness in the workplace, which expressed itself in negative attitudes toward the work. According to J. T. O'Donnell, "Alfie Kohn, in his book, *Punished by Rewards,* argues that millennials have an addiction to praise, perks, and other external incentives, what some call bribes." Therefore, when the newness of the job wears off, there is an expectation the company will fix it with more incentives and fun perks to keep their workers happy.[3]

The expectation that someone else, be it the employer or the company, must fix the problem expresses a failure to look inside and take responsibility for oneself.

Externalizing the Blame

Looking elsewhere for the cause of a problem is nothing new and it is certainly not limited to millennials. The Torah begins by describing this very type of behavior. When Adam disobeys God's command and eats from the Tree of Knowledge, he blames Eve: "The woman whom you gave to be with me, she gave me of the tree and I ate." Eve then does the same thing, pointing her finger at the snake: "The serpent deceived me and I ate."[4] The blame game continues into the next generation, with Adam and Eve's son, Cain. After Cain kills his brother Abel, God asks Cain where Abel is, to which Cain famously responds, "Am I my brother's keeper?"[5] Even Noah, whom the Bible calls "righteous" and who takes responsibility for his own actions, fails to take responsibility for others. It is not until Abraham comes on the scene that we encounter a personality who represents total responsibility, both for his own actions and for others as well. As former British Chief Rabbi, Lord Jonathan Sacks, put it: "With Abraham a new faith is born: the faith of responsibility."[6] Abraham introduces a religion which emphasizes taking personal responsibility, *not* pointing the finger elsewhere.

Rabbi Sacks writes that in the past people blamed their mistakes and flaws on the stars, on fate, and on the gods. Today, we blame our parents, the environment, our genes, the educational system, politicians—on anything and everything but ourselves.

Rabbi Sacks notes three influential thinkers who contributed to this mindset: Benedict Spinoza, Karl Marx, and Sigmund Freud. Each attributed human behavior to other forces they believed were "responsible" for the actions and decisions we make in life. Marx argued that man is ultimately a product of social forces, shaped by the ruling class who are the owners of property, most significantly land or real estate. Spinoza believed in genetic determinism, that we are ruled by the innate instincts and biological drives given to us at birth. Finally, Freud taught that the influence of our early years, childhood traumas, and the relationship we had with our parents, particularly our fathers, in the end determine our behavior.

It is to each of these factors and influences, suggests Rabbi Sacks, that God tells Abraham: "Go from your land, from your birthplace and from the house of your father."[7] To the belief we are controlled by economic forces, the ruling class and landowners, God tells Abraham, "go from *your land*." To the belief that our choices are predetermined by genetics, by the way we were born, God tells Abraham, "go from *your birthplace*." And to the notion that our behaviors are fully determined by childhood experiences and by our parents—our fathers—God says, "go from *the house of your father*."

Our parents and childhood experiences no doubt influence our behavior well into our adult lives, but can we truly say they prevent us from exercising free will and are the only factors that determine our behavior? Socioeconomic factors, genetics, and family upbringing play a huge role in developing the way we think and the kinds of decisions we ultimately make, but when God told Abraham, "Go from your land, from your birthplace, and from the house of your father," the Almighty was telling us that although these factors play an important role, nonetheless they do not control our behavior or the decisions we make. Judaism strongly believes in free will, that we *can* go beyond these factors. Pointing our finger at socioeconomic factors or genetics or blaming our parents for our mistakes or poor decision making is just playing the blame game. We need to go beyond our parents or the culture in which we were raised. For sure they play a part, as does our genetic makeup, but ultimately, we must take responsibility for our own actions, if we want to fix a mistake and have true blessings in our life.

If we prevail in externalizing the blame, the Torah teaches, we'll never be great. The very next verse, after God tells Abraham to go beyond these factors, tells us: "And I will make you into a great nation, and I will bless you, and your name will be great and you will be a blessing."[8] The biblical commentator Rashi explained this verse to mean that Abraham would never be able to enjoy the blessings God had in store for him unless he left the place where he grew up. If he allowed himself to be controlled by his childhood influences, Abraham would never have been able to develop into a great nation: "there, I can make you into a great nation, but here, you will never merit children."[9] Children represent the future. If you attribute your failings to your family, your upbringing, or the neighborhood in which you were raised, you will have no future. Playing the blame game will prevent us from becoming the people we have the potential to be. Only when we look to ourselves for the root of our issues and challenges, will we become great people. As long as we point our finger at our parents, our teachers, or the family into which we were born, we keep ourselves from doing the hard work internally to confront and ultimately resolve our most fundamental issues in life.

Literature and film offer countless narratives that show how the hero's journey brings him or her face to face with the hard truths about the influences of their past, compels them to acknowledge the truth, and ultimately take responsibility for their own actions. Each of these stories are metaphors for our own struggle to ensure our past influences do not keep us from fulfilling our destiny.

In the late nineties sci-fi smash-hit, *The Matrix*, after losing a battle to machines, humans are forced to live in a computer-generated matrix. While humans think that they are living in a human reality, their entire existence is an illusion. The hero, Neo, is lured to a run-down apartment where the leader of the resistance, Morpheus, offers Neo a choice of two pills. The blue pill will allow Neo to remain in the world of illusion, preventing him from taking personal responsibility for the situation. The red pill will open his eyes to the true nature of reality in the Matrix—and requires he join the resistance. Neo chooses the red pill. Morpheus reveals to Neo that the city of Zion is the last outpost of humans not programmed to live in the Matrix and tells him that he is "The One" who will lead the rebellion with a coterie of people who have been liberated from the illusory world of the Matrix. Neo is put through a series of tests to see if he is "The One." To become a true leader, Neo had to face the reality about the Matrix.

In *Star Wars*, Luke Skywalker cannot fulfill his greatness until he faces the truth about his past—that the evil Darth Vader is his true father—and can only become his own man by literally and figuratively slaying this influence. In the *Lord of the Rings* trilogy, the hero Aragorn cannot stop the spread of Sauron's evil until he accepts the responsibility of his true calling as a king, accepting the sword of Andúril from Lord Elrond, who tells him to put aside the Ranger and become who he was meant to be.

These stories all teach the same lesson: to be successful we must face the truth and accept responsibility for ourselves. A fascinating study conducted by the University of Pennsylvania compared the top 1 percent of neurosurgeons in America with the bottom 1 percent. The top 1 percent of neurosurgeons are the leading researchers in the country and some of the most sought-after physicians in the world, whereas the bottom 1 percent includes some of the worst doctors, many of whom have been fired or sued for malpractice. The study concluded that what distinguished these two groups from one another was not necessarily the medical schools they attended or the level of intelligence of the individual physicians, but rather how the doctors handled mistakes in the operating room. The study showed how after mistakes or failures took place, the top 1 percent of neurosurgeons tried to determine where *they themselves* went wrong versus the bottom 1 percent who attributed their patient's demise to hospital equipment, nursing staff, poor lighting in the operating room . . . everything except for themselves. The bottom 1 percent pointed the finger elsewhere. They externalized the blame, whereas the top 1 percent took responsibility and looked inside for the causes.

How often do *we* do this in our own lives?

When a relationship starts to break down, do we ask what *we ourselves* are doing that may be contributing to the problem? When a deal at work goes south or if, as an attorney, you lose a case, do you accept responsibility or is your first reaction to blame someone else? Examine any case of corporate malfeasance and corruption—from Enron to Arthur Andersen to Lehman Brothers—and you will find buck passing, avoidance of consequences, and excuses. The same is true of doping scandals, political crimes, and environmental accidents—a culture where no one takes responsibility.

If we play the blame game, chances are we'll also probably make the same mistake again. Some of the fault may, in fact, lie with someone else, but even if we are just partially at fault, something we did or didn't do *contributed* to the mistake. If we never take the time to look inside, we rob ourselves of the opportunity to truly fix the problem and grow from a negative situation, perhaps the very reason we were confronted with the situation to begin with.

"My Bad"

Accepting responsibility and saying the words *my bad* is never easy, but it's the only way to grow. Pointing the finger elsewhere, or admitting fault, but justifying it by saying "that's just the way I was raised," or "what else can you expect from someone with my background?" is ultimately an abdication of human responsibility and a guaranteed way of repeating the mistake.

This lesson is very powerfully made by one of the most unlikely figures in the Bible, Achashverosh, King of Ancient Persia. Achashverosh's

Prime Minister Haman manages to convince the king to approve his evil plot to annihilate all the Jews living in the Persian Kingdom. The beautiful Esther, the Jewess chosen to be Achashverosh's queen, throws two parties for the king and invites Haman to each one. After the second party, the Bible tells us Achashverosh was having a hard time falling asleep: "on that night the sleep of the king was disturbed."[10] The king orders one of his servants to bring him the book of chronicles, which records all the doings of the king. Rashi, the biblical commentator, calls this a "miracle." After having the book read to him, the king learns that Mordechai the Jew had foiled an assassination attempt against the king's life but had never been rewarded for his act of patriotism. Achashverosh then commands his servant to reward Mordechai, which becomes the first act in the reversal of the course of events ultimately leading to the saving of the Jewish people.

Why couldn't Achashverosh sleep and why did he ask his servant to bring him his book of chronicles? Finally, why does Rashi call this a miracle? What is miraculous about a king who couldn't sleep and therefore summons his servant to bring him something to read? The Talmud sage Rava answered that Achashverosh was tossing and turning because he couldn't understand why Esther kept inviting Haman to the parties she was throwing. Was she conspiring with Haman against him? If so, Achashverosh asked himself: "wasn't there anyone who cares enough about me to let me know what's going on behind my back?"

But then, "he thought again," says the Talmud, "perhaps there is someone who did me a favor, maybe there are people who cared enough to help but I never rewarded them and because of this people refrain from helping and informing me of such matters."[11] These thoughts move Achashverosh to call to his servant: "get me the book of chronicles!"[12] Perhaps someone had tried to help me, Achashverosh considered to himself, and had never been rewarded. Maybe that's why no one is helping me now!

Rabbi Dr. Norman Lamm suggests that although Achashverosh is not seen by Jewish tradition in a positive light, he did something quite admirable: he took personal responsibility for his actions. Instead of blaming everyone around him, the Persian king told himself: maybe *I* failed in some way! Maybe *I* didn't react to other people's help in the right manner and maybe that's why no one is helping me now! In Rabbi Lamm's words: "The royal insomnia became a creative challenge. He converted it from a suspicion of plots by others to a discovery of shortcomings within himself."[13] *That* was the miracle to which Rashi referred, that someone whom Jewish tradition considers a fool or even wicked could go from thinking that the fault lay in something external to something within his own self. And it's all captured in the Talmudic phrase: *he thought again.* After Achashverosh imagined it was everyone else's fault, "he thought again" and considered the possibility that the fault lay with him. This level of honesty was rare among Persian kings and remains rare among the "kings" and "queens" of today, but is certainly something to which we should ideally aspire.

We all have things that keep us up late at night, thoughts that disturb our sleep and cause us to toss and turn. Sometimes there's nothing we can do about the situation because the fault lies with someone else, but, more often than not, some of the fault lies within ourselves. It could be a situation at work, where we are convinced that our troubling work situation lies with a difficult co-worker or with an uncompromising boss, but we need to ask: What am *I* doing to feed the situation? Am *I* somehow contributing to the negative dynamic, and if so, what can *I* do to change things? We can't control other people's behavior, but we can start with our own. Often that acknowledgment or change in our own behavior helps encourage others, who may also be part of the problem, to make a change too.

If a relationship isn't working out it could just be that the relationship was not meant to be. It could also be that the other person has acted inappropriately, but it is likely that our actions or our attitude are also contributing in some way. Given the frustrations we all experience in the realm of relationship building, we owe it to ourselves to ask: *what can I do differently?* It can be a difficult question to ask, but posing that honest question may save the relationship.

What can I do differently?

I believe we also need to ask this question when it comes to our religious lives. Ours is a generation that feels spiritually disconnected. We wonder why we're not feeling as connected to God, to our religious heritage, or even to the other members of our spiritual community. It may be true that there are lots of people who may have turned us off to religion, or perhaps we were never exposed to the most positive of religious experiences in our childhood. But we must consider what responsibility lies with us too. What am *I* doing to feel more connected? Am *I* truly making efforts to feel more spiritually connected or am I just expecting to feel something without putting in the work?

And if I am putting in effort, am I simply doing the same thing today as I did yesterday? I always say to my students: Torah is to the soul like a drug is to the body. Just like the body gets used to certain drugs, and therefore one must vary the medication for the body to continue to be impacted, as we mature and develop, our soul also needs more to stay connected to its Divine source. This is therefore why we always need to be growing and developing ourselves spiritually—always learning something new or finding a deeper insight into something of which we are already aware. In the Jewish faith, this could mean taking on a new mitzvah (precept of the Torah) or deepening our understanding and commitment to those mitzvoth we may already be observing. Otherwise we become lethargic and sluggish. We stagnate and we become unhappy. But the solution starts with looking inside. We could easily point to all sorts of external factors responsible for our spiritual stagnation: the rabbi isn't sufficiently inspiring, my Jewish educational background is too limited, my friends aren't interested in being spiritually involved. All are legitimate "reasons" for not pushing ourselves forward, but at the end of the day we cannot control other people and we can't change the past. We need to get beyond the external factors and follow Achashverosh's example of "he thought again," always asking ourselves: what could *we* do differently?

The next time something goes wrong, be it at work, in a relationship, or in your spiritual connection, instead of looking elsewhere, look within. Leave behind the external factors and explore what you may be doing to contribute to the situation. God's command to Abraham, "lech lecha" literally means "Go into *you*." Leave the external and *go into yourself* because that's where you will find the root of the problem, and hopefully the solution.

Notes

1. Geoff Pound, "Starting Over," *Stories for Speakers and Writers*, May 17, 2006, http://storiesforspeakers.blogspot.com/2006/05/starting-over.html?m=0.
2. Nikki Krize, "UPDATE: Danville Students to Face Alcohol-Related Charges," WNEP, May 7, 2013, http://wnep.com/2013/05/07/danville-students-to-face-alcohol-related-charges/.
3. J.T. O'Donnell, "3 Reasons Millennials Are Getting Fired," *Inc.*, August 4, 2015, http://www.inc.com/jt-odonnell/3-reasons-millennials-are-getting-fired.html.
4. Genesis 3:12–13.
5. Genesis 4:9.
6. Rabbi Lord Jonathan Sacks, *Covenant & Conversation*, Jerusalem, Israel: Maggid Books, 2009), 68.
7. Genesis 12:1.
8. Genesis 12:2.
9. Rashi on Genesis 12:2.
10. Esther 6:1.
11. Talmud, Megillah 15b.
12. Esther 6:1.
13. Sermon entitled "The Royal Insomnia" delivered March 9, 1963 at the Jewish Center, New York, on website called: "The Lamm Heritage," https://www.yu.edu/about/lamm-heritage.

Chapter 6

GOING FROM OBJECT TO SUBJECT

Sixth Commandment: Thou Shalt Take Control

Jackie Robinson graduated UCLA as the only student to win varsity letters in basketball, football, track, and baseball. He was great at virtually every sport. Jackie's older brother had won a medal in the 1936 Olympics, but as a black man returning to Pasadena, he could only find work as a garbage man. This made a huge impact on Jackie's determination to make it as a black man in what was then the all-white sport of baseball. With the Negro Leagues as the only opportunity to play professional baseball, Jackie joined the Kansas City Monarchs, but in the same year was recruited by the Brooklyn Dodgers. As the only black man on the team, Jackie was subject to lots of derision and bigotry. Determined to make it as a professional baseball player, Jackie never responded to the jeers and bigoted remarks players and fans would continually make as he would walk into the batter's box. Despite the threats and racial slurs, Jackie simply continued to play and impress people with his athleticism and unimpeachable moral integrity. The object of endless ridicule and nasty, bigoted comments, he never gave in to the lowly remarks and proved himself more than worthy of the sport, leading the Brooklyn Dodgers to win the 1955 World Series against the New York Yankees. Even after he retired from baseball, Robinson continued to fight on behalf of civil rights, working alongside the great Reverend Dr. Martin Luther King.

Despite being placed in what seemed like a helpless situation, completely out of his control, Robinson's extraordinary self-restraint and discipline transformed him from *object to subject*, fulfilling one of the most profound teachings of the Torah.

In the book of Genesis, the Bible describes three incidents that take place in the life of the biblical character Joseph. In the very next chapter each of those incidents is repeated: The first incident involves dreams. In chapter 37 of the Book of Genesis, Joseph tells of his two dreams to his brothers and later in chapter 40 the Torah describes Joseph interpreting the dreams of his two cellmates in prison.

The second incident concerns "the pit." In chapter 37 of Genesis, the Torah describes Joseph being thrown into a pit by his brothers, and in chapter 39 Joseph is thrown into an Egyptian prison (which the Bible calls a *pit*) from which he ultimately rises to royalty.

The third incident involves temptation and includes a second biblical figure, Judah—one of Joseph's older brothers. In chapter 38, Tamar, the wife of Judah's eldest son, dresses up like a prostitute and tempts her father-in-law, Judah, and later in chapter 39 Joseph resists the temptations and sexual advances of the wife of Potiphar.

What is the significance of all this repetition?

My friend and colleague Rabbi Yosie Levine, rabbi of the Jewish Center, suggested that each situation demonstrates Joseph's transformation from *object to subject*. In each of these three situations Joseph is first acted upon—he begins as a passive object, but ultimately exerts his own influence and takes control of the situation.

In the first instance, Joseph begins by merely *telling* his dreams to his brothers (which only gets him into trouble) but later he takes to *interpreting* other people's dreams. In helping others make sense of their troubling dreams, Joseph develops a reputation as an effective dream interpreter which inspires Pharaoh to fetch him from jail to interpret his own troubling dreams. Pharaoh is so impressed with Joseph and his dream interpretation he releases him from prison and appoints him viceroy of Egypt.

In the second situation, Joseph is simply thrown into a pit by his angry brothers and then sold into slavery. Later when Joseph again finds himself in "the pit," this time in an Egyptian prison cell, Joseph reaches out to his cell mates, offers them help, and it is here where he develops his reputation as a dream interpreter. Instead of simply feeling sorry for himself he turns to his cell mates and asks: "Why do you look so upset today?"[1] Overcoming the natural tendency to become absorbed in one's own problems, Joseph turns to his neighbor and opens a dialogue. By asking them what was troubling them and offering them aid he transforms the second pit scenario into a positive situation by turning away from the role of victim to that of leader.

In the third scenario Judah gives into temptation, submitting to a prostitute who, unbeknownst to him, was his own daughter-in-law Tamar. Later we see Joseph in a similar situation, the object of his master Potiphar's wife's sexual advances. In this case however, unlike his brother Judah, Joseph resists the temptation. He fights off the urge to be with Potiphar's wife, which the Jewish Sages describe as a heroic feat. Potiphar's wife was very beautiful and relentless. "Each and every day," the Talmud says, "the wife of Potiphar would attempt to seduce him with words. Clothes she wore for him in the morning, she would not wear for him in the evening. Clothes she wore for him in the evening, she would not wear for him in the morning. She said to him, 'Surrender yourself to me.' He answered her, 'No.' She threatened him, 'I shall confine you in prison . . . I shall bend your proud stature . . . I will blind your eyes . . . ,' but Joseph refused her. She then offered him a huge sum of money, but he did not budge."[2]

Joseph does not allow himself to fall victim to circumstances and instead takes control of the situation by refusing to give in. In this scenario and in the two others Joseph transforms himself from *object to subject*, asserting a level of control over the situation in which he finds himself.

Modern Day Examples

There are many contemporary examples of the biblical Joseph, individuals who refuse to become passive victims of circumstance and who transform themselves from object to subject. Consider Arizona Congresswoman Gabby Gifford, shot in the head in Tucson during an assassination attempt by Jared Loughner. Gifford persevered through a long and grueling recovery and, while she still suffers from speech and ambulatory limitations, she has taken leadership of a national campaign to reduce gun violence in America. Gifford could have played the victim and retreated into a life of solitude and personal pity, but instead she invested her energies into making the world safer.

Another modern-day example is research scientist Eleanor Longden. Diagnosed with a devastating case of schizophrenia, Longden was tormented and nearly driven to violence and suicide by voices generated by her illness. She was hospitalized, drugged, and discarded by a system that didn't know how to help her. Longden was eventually empowered by a psychiatrist to understand the voices in her head not as her enemies but as "a source of insight into solvable emotional problems."[3] Since then she has earned a doctorate, published a book, and works with victims of schizophrenia, helping them find the peace she finally found for herself.

French Journalist Jean Dominique Barbais, after a massive stroke, was left completely paralyzed except for the ability to blink his left eyelid. Refusing to be the victim, he went on to write a bestselling book, blinking out one word at a time. Shawn Swarener was diagnosed with cancer at the age of sixteen and was given two weeks to live, yet he somehow managed to climb Mt. Everest with only partial use of his lungs. He simply refused to allow his illness to hold him back. We're all familiar with the more well-known examples of Nelson Mandela and Mahatma Gandhi who used their imprisonment as the impetus to fight for basic human freedoms. Or human rights activist Malala Yousafzai, who stood up against the Taliban for women's education and was shot in an attempted assassination. She refused to be silenced and put her life back together to become a world leader for peace and education and winner of the Nobel Peace Prize. "I don't want to be remembered as the girl who was shot," she has said. "I want to be remembered as the girl who stood up."

These extraordinary people embody the life lesson of the biblical Joseph: someone who began his life as the ultimate victim of circumstance—a teenager whose brothers had thrown him into a pit and sold him into slavery—but who eventually developed himself into a master of his own fate. In their comments on Joseph's descent to Egypt, the Jewish Sages make the following remark: "'And Joseph was brought down to Egypt'—don't read that Joseph was brought down to Egypt but that he brought down others, namely his father and brothers."[4]

Although Joseph found himself in Egypt as an object of other people's manipulation, the Jewish Sages want us to focus on how Joseph changed that dynamic and took control of the situation. Joseph does this by bringing his family down to Egypt. This move not only saved his family from the raging famine in Israel, but it also began a family reunification and reconciliation after their many years of discord, also vital for the future of the Jewish people.

Transforming ourselves from object to subject is a fundamental Jewish teaching necessary for happiness on both the personal and national levels. Figuring out a way to change a difficult dynamic in which we find ourselves, so we can assert control over our circumstances, is vital for both personal happiness and freedom on the national level.

The revered Rabbi Joseph B. Soloveitchick taught that this is precisely what was accomplished by the modern Zionist movement. For two thousand years, the Jew had been victim to the control and dominance of other peoples and governments. As visitors in other people's land, Jews has been the object of dominators' manipulation and control. By creating a presence and ultimately sovereignty in the land of their forefathers, Rabbi Soloveitchick argued the modern-day Zionist movement effectively transformed the Jewish people from a people of *fate*, subject to the whims of other rulers, to a people of *destiny* capable of chartering and shaping their own future. While a life of fate is thrust upon the group or individual, a life of destiny is freely chosen by the people of their own volition.

Rabbi Soloveitchik taught that one of the fundamental goals of human existence is to transform ourselves from objects to subjects. From an existence where things are simply happening *to us* to one where we take control and *we* become the actors. For many years, my email signature had this quote from Rabbi Soloveitchik: "Man's task in the world, according to Judaism, is to transform fate into destiny; a passive existence into an active existence; an existence of compulsion, perplexity and muteness into an existence replete with a powerful will, with resourcefulness, daring, and imagination."[5]

The best *ancient* example of this, again on the national level, was the story of the Jews living under Greek rule. The Jewish community, living under the Greek Seleucid Empire in the year 167 BCE, was placed in what seemed to be an impossibly helpless position. Subject to the mighty Greek forces ruling over ancient Judea, Jews were faced with an impossible choice: relinquish their practice of Judaism in favor of the prevailing Hellenistic culture or suffer death at the hands of the more powerful Greek forces. Many Jews began to abandon their Judaism, changing their names and covering up their circumcisions to look and sound as Greek as possible. Others faced martyrdom and paid the ultimate price. However, another group of Jews, the Hasmonites, better known as the Macabees, refused to accept the Greek ultimatum of abandoning Judaism or facing death. Instead they created a third option: revolt! The Macabees staged a difficult but ultimately successful revolt against the mightier Greek forces. In refusing to choose between the options the Greeks tried imposing upon them and instead revolting, the Jewish community took the situation into their own hands and transformed themselves from object to subject, a powerful theme Jews celebrate each year on the Hanukkah holiday.

Remaining victim to circumstance and allowing others to control a people's destiny is something against which groups throughout history have fought. The human impulse for freedom demands that a nation charter its own course. On the individual level, controlling one's own destiny is no less important to finding personal happiness and fulfillment.

Combating Helplessness

In studies of "learned helplessness," animals that are repeatedly exposed to painful stimuli which they cannot escape will eventually stop trying to avoid the stimulus and behave as if they are helpless to change their situation—even when opportunities to escape become available. After the animal "learns" to become helpless, it will choose to remain helpless to free itself. The only cure, discovered through these studies, is to show the animals through physical contact and aid that they *can* remove themselves from the situation. By providing outside empowerment, the animals learn that they are *not* helpless and that they are in fact capable of saving themselves from suffering.

Within the human realm, victims of abuse often suffer from this learned helplessness, and endure abuse even when they can escape it. There is also a direct correlation between depression and learned helplessness, which then makes breaking free even more difficult.[6]

As evident from the examples I cited earlier, our world is full of examples of real people who have broken free of mental illness and other misfortunes which would have rendered any one of us a victim of circumstance. The point is clear: we can become convinced we have no way out of a situation when in fact the solution or some way out is right before us.

Have you experienced times when you became convinced you had no choice but to remain the *object* of someone else's control? Have you seen yourself as a victim of circumstances, over which you could do nothing but submit to someone else's authority? It could be a situation at work where we are subjected to the inappropriate or abusive talk of a superior. We may *feel* we have no choice but to simply take the abuse or risk losing an otherwise good job. However, in reality, we may have other choices. We may be able to stand up to our boss and still hold on to the job, and maybe even demand more respect in the process. I know someone who worked at a university where his boss made subtle but unmistakably racist comments about Black and Jewish students. At first my friend thought he had no power to object without putting his own job in jeopardy. However, after speaking with some friends and a lawyer, he realized his boss was actually out on a limb, and could never publicly or privately defend those remarks. My friend realized he had the high ground.

We always have other choices. We can blow the whistle on abusive or sexually predatory behavior on the part of a boss and change the world for the better. It happened with Harvey Weinstein of Miramax, whose sexual harassment was well-known among many women who worked near or around him. When victims stepped up to challenge him legally, others also emerged and he was fired. People stopped acting as subjects of abuse and a bully was taken down.

Remaining in an abusive situation is always a choice, and as much as we may desperately need the job, we must consider the negative effects of remaining in such a position. Staying an object can be more detrimental to us than we think.

The same goes for romantic relationships: one of my students complained to me about her boyfriend whom she had been dating seriously for over two years. Every time she brought up the topic of marriage he changed the subject or would pull away from her. My student felt if she continued to pressure him he would bolt, and she really loved him. She felt like she had no choice but to remain in the relationship and simply hope he would have a change of heart. I sympathized with her situation, but I told her she was being an object and that she needed to transform herself into the subject by taking control of the situation. I told her she needed to believe in herself more and to tell her boyfriend, in the sweetest way possible, that she could no longer remain in the relationship if he couldn't make a commitment. Leaving someone we love brings us pain, yes, but ultimately what is more human? As John Irving observed in the seminal *The World According to Garp*, loving can someday mean you will be "involved in that awkward procedure of getting to unknow each other." By leaving, we affirm we believe that love can happen to us again. "Grief is in two parts," wrote the novelist Anne Roiphe. "The first is loss. The second is the remaking of life." Theologian Henri Nouwen wrote, "Still, if we want to avoid the suffering of leaving, we will never experience the joy of loving. And love is stronger than fear, life stronger than death, hope stronger than despair. We have to trust that the risk of loving is always worth taking."

One gentleman called me to tell me that his daughter, a young woman raised in a very religious Jewish home, was told by her boyfriend that if she wouldn't be physically intimate with him, he would break up with her. The father asked me how I thought he should counsel his daughter. In classic Jewish tradition, I answered his question with one of my own: "Is that the kind of husband your daughter really wants to have?" But to our point, I also encouraged him to advise his daughter not to submit to such an ultimatum because that would be allowing herself to be treated as an object. In reality, this young woman had more control over her situation than she thought. She felt trapped wanting to make the relationship work, but as I explained to her and others in similar situations, there is something worse than being alone: staying in an abusive relationship. Remaining in a relationship whereby one is somehow manipulated to behave against one's wishes or conscience is allowing oneself to be the object of another's abuse.

The most important thing is not to allow oneself to feel helpless and trapped. We may think or feel we have no room to assert any control, but we often have more options then we think.

Natan Sharansky

In his extraordinary book, *Fear No Evil*, former Soviet dissident (and my personal hero) Natan Sharansky tells of his experiences in a Soviet prison after he was arrested for Zionist activities and for "spying for America."

The holiday of Hanukkah was approaching. Sharansky explained to his friends in prison that there was this Jewish holiday which celebrated his people's national freedom and retaining their own distinct culture in the face of forced assimilation. Sharansky's cell mates were so impressed with the holiday they decided to celebrate Hanukkah with Natan and even fashioned a wooden menorah from materials in the prison. The prisoners found some candles and on the first night Sharansky lit the menorah and afterwards shared the heroic struggle of the Maccabees with his prison mates.

This Hanukkah celebration continued each night for the next several days, until one of the cell mates, a man by the name of Gavriliuk (a Soviet collaborator whose bunk was across from Sharansky), began to grumble: "Look at him, he made himself a synagogue. And what if there's a fire?"[7] On the sixth night of Hanukkah the authorities confiscated Natan's menorah with all the candles. They said the candles were made from state materials and therefore were illegal and that other prisoners were complaining he may start a fire. Sharansky complained to the Soviet authorities: "In two days Hanukkah will be over and then I'll return this 'state property' to you. Now, however, this looks like an attempt to deny me the opportunity of celebrating Jewish holidays." He received the following response from the authorities: "A camp is not a synagogue. We won't permit Sharansky to pray here."[8]

In protest, Sharansky declared a hunger strike against what he said was a violation of his national and religious rights, and against the KGB's interference in his personal life. He didn't know this at the time, but in a few weeks a commission from Moscow was due to arrive in the camp, which explains why just two days into the hunger strike Sharansky was summoned to the office of the head of the prison, Major Osin. Sharansky describes Major Osin as a huge, burly man who "seemed to have long ago lost interest in everything but food." Osin tried talking Sharansky out of his hunger strike and promised to personally guarantee that in the future nobody would hinder him from praying.

"Then what's the problem?" Sharansky asked. "Give me back the menorah, as tonight is the last evening of Hanukkah. Let me celebrate it, now and . . . I shall end the hunger strike."[9] But the protocol of confiscation had already been executed and Osin couldn't back down in front of the entire camp.

"Listen," Sharansky said, "I'm sure you have the menorah somewhere. It's very important to me to celebrate the last night of Hanukkah. Why not let me do it here and now, together with you? You'll give me the menorah, I'll light the candles and say the prayer, and if all goes well I'll end the hunger strike."

Osin thought it over and promptly retrieved the confiscated menorah from his desk. He summoned Gavriliuk, who was on duty in the office, to bring in a large candle.

"I need eight candles," Sharansky said.

Sharansky continued: "Osin took out a handsome inlaid pocketknife and deftly cut me eight candles. I arranged the candles and went to the coat-rack for my hat, explaining to Osin that 'during the prayer you must stand with your head covered and at the end say 'Amen.'" Osin put on his major's hat and stood. "I lit the candles and recited my own prayer in Hebrew, which went something like this: 'Blessed are You, Ado-nai, for allowing me to rejoice on this day of Hanukkah, the holiday of our liberation, the holiday of our return to the way of our fathers. Blessed are You, Ado-nai, for allowing me to light these candles. May you allow me to light the Hanukkah candles many times in your city, Jerusalem, with my wife, Avital, and my family and friends.'"

Inspired by the sight of Osin standing meekly at attention, Sharansky added in Hebrew: "And may the day come when all our enemies, who today are planning our destruction, will stand before us and hear our prayers and say 'Amen.'"

"Amen," Osin echoed back.[10]

I can think of no greater example of someone completely helpless and subject to another's control than a prisoner in the Soviet gulag. Yet, even in that extreme predicament, Sharansky managed to assert some level of control over his situation. Like the modern Zionist movement today, the ancient Jewish community in Greek times, and the biblical Joseph, Natan Sharansky managed to go from *object to subject* and in doing so became a master of his own destiny.

Transforming a life of fate into one of destiny gives us the upper hand in life and prevents other forces from simply moving us from one place to another like a feather in the wind. On both the individual and national level we are often moved by circumstances from one predicament to another, but that only happens when we allow it. Whether in our personal lives or on the national level, we must find an alternative route which allows us to take control of the situation.

In our own time, we have been witness to the Jewish people rising from the ashes of the Holocaust to the creation of the modern state of Israel. A people who, in one decade were the object of another people's manipulation and abuse, became masters of their own fate in another. Following this example in our own personal lives by transforming our situations from *object to subject* is necessary to living a life of destiny and vital to finding true happiness.

Notes

1. Genesis 40:7.
2. Talmud, Yoma 36a.
3. Emily Pate, "Hearing voices in your head: A sane survival strategy for dealing with past trauma," *Rooted in Rights*, December 3, 2014, http://www.rootedinrights.org/hearing-voices-in-your-head-a-sane-survival-strategy-for-dealing-with-past-trauma/.
4. Midrash Tanchuma, Parshat Vayeshev Section 4.
5. Rabbi Joseph B. Soloveitchik, *Fate and Destiny* (Hoboken, NJ: Ktav Publishing House, 2000), 6.
6. "How Learned Helplessness Damages Victims, By A Guest Blogger," *Wheatish Complexion*, November 30, 2014, http://www.wheatishcomplexion.com/how-learned-helplessness-damages-victims-by-a-guest-blogger/.
7. Natan Sharansky, *Fear No Evil* (New York: Random House, 1988), 306.
8. Ibid.
9. Ibid, 307.
10. Ibid, 308.

Chapter 7

WHAT'S YOUR MISSION?

Seventh Commandment: *Thou Shalt Make a Difference*

An older gentleman was sitting in a restaurant in Kansas City. Another man about two tables away kept looking at him until he finally recognized him. He got up and walked over to the table and said, "You're Captain Plumb."

The older man looked up and said, "Yes, sir, I'm Captain Plumb."

"You were a Top Gun fighter pilot and flew jet fighters in Vietnam. You were on the aircraft carrier *Kitty Hawk*. You were shot down. You parachuted into enemy hands and spent six years as a prisoner of war."

"How in the world did you know all that?" asked the older man.

"Because I was the guy who packed your parachute."

Captain Plumb rose to his feet and held out his hand. "Thank you for packing my parachute."

"I guess it worked," the other man said.

"Yes, sir, indeed it did," Plumb said, "and I guess I have you to thank for my life."

Captain Plumb thought to himself: "Here's a sailor well below the water line of the aircraft carrier. He stands at a long wooden table and weaves the shrouds and folds the silks of these parachutes while jet jockey, the Top Gun, zooms around the sky at twice the speed of sound. I couldn't have cared less about the guy down there in the hole, until one day my parachute came along and he packed mine up for me."[1]

We are all enamored with Top Gun jet fighters, but aren't the sailors down below packing the parachutes just as important? Can we really say one is more important than the other?

Research shows that people at any level of skill are happiest with work that not only challenges them, but provides a sense of purpose and mission at work. One famous analysis of 400,000 workers found that autonomy and control over one's life and work process matter more to happiness than money. People with high income but little autonomy are less happy than people with a low income but control over what they do. The research demonstrated that if you can find ways of aligning your life and work with your individual purpose, you can be happy even on a lower income.[2] These studies corroborate the importance of mission and belonging in our work.

The biblical book of Samuel reveals this truth through the story of the conflict between the first ever King of Israel, King Saul, and the young hero, David. Saul was increasingly jealous of David, whose popularity he considered a threat to his throne, so much so that David feared for his life. David turned to his best friend Jonathan for help. Jonathan, who was Saul's eldest son, tells David he would try to get a sense from his father, but meanwhile advises David to hide. Jonathan tells David that in three days he will come to the large field ostensibly to practice his archery. He suggests David hide behind the big stone "Azel" and wait there until he comes with the *na'ar*, his young servant. Jonathan will then shoot three arrows in David's direction, as if he were shooting at a target, after which he will send the young servant to find the arrows. Jonathan tells David that if he shoots the arrows so that they fall short of where he is hiding, that is a sign that all is well and he can come out of hiding, but if he shoots the arrows beyond the rock where David is hiding, then that's the signal Saul seeks to destroy him and that he must quickly flee.[3]

That was the plan, anyway.

At the palace feast King Saul creates a scene and accuses his son Jonathan of plotting with David and condemns David to death as a traitor. The next morning Jonathan goes with the *na'ar*, the young servant, aims his arrows well beyond where David was secretly stationed and tells his servant to go farther since the arrow is still farther on. When David sees the lad running he realizes he must hide, which he does until Saul is told by God he is no longer King and David is eventually crowned King of Israel.

Who are the main characters in this story?

Most of us would probably say Saul, David, or Jonathan. But what about the *na'ar*, the young servant? What about the boy sent to run after the arrows? What part did he play?

Rabbi Dr. Lamm makes the point that if it wasn't for the lad, who knew nothing of the great drama that was unfolding, David may never have become King of Israel and ultimately the ancestor of our Messiah. Without the lad and his running after the arrows, David could have been discovered and killed and ultimately his ascendancy to the throne of Israel would never have taken place.

The *na'ar* in fact plays a vital role. But our natural reaction is to focus on the big people, the "important" ones: Saul, David, and Jonathan. Our tendency is to overlook the others, and we're doing this more today than ever before. When I was growing up there was *one* program, *Lifestyles of the Rich and Famous*, which gave us a glimpse into the life of those we considered more important. Today there are countless shows that enable us to see how the "important" people live—you know, the ones with the money and influence. Truthfully it does us all a real disservice as it reinforces the false belief that only some people matter and only *their* lives are worth watching and emulating.

In Jewish thought, there's no such thing as an unimportant life, or an insignificant role for any human being. We all matter because each of us, whether we drive a cab or cure cancer—whether we're the young servant in the book of Samuel or the sailor making parachutes—each of us has a role to play and each of those roles is important in the end. The only question is: do we recognize the role each of us plays and do we value it?

A young man once attended his first classical music concert with twenty-two musicians playing in the symphony. He watched the musicians swaying back and forth as they played their instruments with passion and excitement, except for one musician, the percussionist, who seemed to be doing almost nothing. Occasionally the percussionist would clang two cymbals together or pick up a triangle and lightly tap on it. After the symphony, the young spectator was brought backstage where the orchestra was packing up. He walked over to the percussionist and bluntly asked, "Is it possible that you earn the same salary as the rest of the musicians?" The percussionist responded, "I may not make what the others make, but without my contribution it's not same piece of music."

The percussionist took his role seriously, realizing the significance of what he was doing. He may not have looked like he was working as hard or contributing as much as the others, but he too had his role. We tend to overlook those who aren't making as much noise but *everyone* has a mission, both in the material and spiritual world.

If you're a teacher or social worker, physician, nurse or therapist, it's probably easier to see how your life is devoted to helping people and therefore you may feel more of a sense of mission and purpose from what you do professionally. But if you work in the financial world or as an attorney and you spend your day poring over contracts, it's important to recognize your work is also necessary for the entire symphony of the economy and for so much else in this world to happen.

The same applies in the spiritual realm. None of us are here accidentally. Each of us was created for a specific purpose with a unique mission to carry out. The following true story makes this point quite powerfully.

The Priest and His Jewish Student

A young Jewish man applied to the Catholic University of America, and the priest conducting the interview informed the young man the school had decided to accept him, but asked for a favor: "Could we meet each week to study the Bible, specifically the Old Testament with Rashi's commentary?"

The student was taken aback by the request. After all, he had never studied the Hebrew Bible before, never having attended a Jewish school. But he thought to himself, "Why not?" and for the next four years the priest and Jewish student met every week to study the Hebrew Bible with Rashi's commentary. At the end of college, before the young man was to graduate, he finally asked the priest, "Why did you want to study Torah with me all these years?" The priest answered the student, "When I was younger I took off a year to go to Israel and immerse myself in Bible studies. On one occasion, I went to visit the Western Wall. It was the Jewish Sabbath and someone approached me and asked if I'd like to join a local Jewish family for a Sabbath meal. I was hungry and so I accepted the invitation. I had lunch at a rabbi's home—his name was Rabbi Noach Weinberg, the head of a large yeshiva in Israel called Aish HaTorah. I was impressed with the rabbi's intellectual sophistication, his deep knowledge of the Bible, and especially his warmth. The rabbi invited me to study in his yeshiva, which I did for an entire year. At the end of the year, when it was time for me to return to America, I went to thank the good rabbi for his help and hospitality. He asked why I couldn't stay in Israel to continue my studies in the Yeshiva and I told him: 'I need to return to the States to continue my Catholic studies to become a priest.'"

The rabbi was not very happy and he told the priest the following: "Promise you'll do something for me. One day a Jew will no doubt come to study at your seminary: promise me you'll teach him what we taught you here."

"Teaching you," the priest continued, "was my way of keeping my promise to the good rabbi."

That young Jewish man, after leaving the University and his years of studying with the priest, continued to study Torah and eventually became a very learned and ultimately an observant Jew.

The priest was what Jewish tradition calls a *shaliach*, a messenger, an emissary, and no doubt sent to help that young Jewish student on his spiritual journey.

We all have a *shlichut*, a mission that we are supposed to carry out in our lives. *Every* person has a mission, not just world leaders, famous actors, or people with lots of money. Our society has shined such a spotlight on people of wealth and fame that too many of us ordinary citizens have stopped viewing ourselves as having a mission and purpose.

But we may have it all wrong. The Talmud tells the story about the Talmudic sage, Rav Yosef, who took ill and slipped into a coma. When he eventually regained consciousness, his father asked him, "What did you see in the next world?" Rav Yosef answered, "I saw an upside-down world. Those on the top of this world are on the bottom and the lowly of this world are on top in that world."[4]

The Real Heroes

The real heroes and people of worth are not always those who are famous or well known. For example, when you think of who was responsible for creating the modern State of Israel, people like Theodore Herzl and David Ben-Gurion come to mind. Herzl and Ben-Gurion were extraordinary Jewish leaders and visionaries who no doubt contributed greatly to the creation of the Jewish State, but Israel was also built by a guy named Murray from Queens. I mean that quite literally. For many years, on the MJE trip I lead to Israel each summer, I brought the group to meet an older gentleman named Murray Greenfield from Far Rockaway, Queens. At the age of seventeen, instead of going to Hunter College to meet girls (as he likes to say), Murray traveled instead to Palestine to smuggle Holocaust survivors from Europe into Israel because the British were refusing entry to Jews. Murray risked his life and was ultimately imprisoned by the British in Atlit where the British imprisoned illegal immigrants.

Every summer I also arrange for my students to hear from another gentleman by the name of David Sprung. David made *aliyah* (immigrated to Israel) from the United States in 1966 when he was eighteen and the next year he was drafted into the army to fight in the Six Day War. He participated in and witnessed some of the most incredible modern-day battlefield miracles, which I believe he merited because of his great devotion to the Jewish people.

Who are these people? Most people have never heard of Murray Greenfield or David Sprung, but they played an instrumental role in the creation of modern Israel as did Theodore Herzl and David Ben-Gurion. The roles they played may not have been as prominent or well-known, but they also served critical functions.

We need to stop assessing people's worth and purpose by their wealth, status, or fame and this applies equally to our spiritual lives. Over the years, I've gotten calls from people who tell me they are not in the practice of praying, but ask whether I could pray for something they really want in life. I always respond positively, but wonder why they feel that my prayers are somehow more important than their own. I always say something like, "You know, God needs to hear your prayers too—the Almighty and the world needs *your* unique spiritual energy and connection, something which cannot be replicated by anyone else."

The great biblical commentator and Kabbalist, Rabbi Chaim ibn Attar, known as the *Ohr Hachayim*, wrote that every human being contains a physical and spiritual component to his or her existence and every Jew possesses a third dimension, namely: "a portion of Torah betrothed to every Jew." If one does not use his or her special part of Torah, continues the *Ohr Hachayim*, it becomes "lost from the world."[5]

But why is this? Why can't someone who has more of an appreciation for Judaism simply use another person's portion of Torah, especially if they will not be "using it" themselves?

No two souls are alike and everyone is given a unique spiritual mission. Therefore, their special portion of Torah needs to be used by that person and that person alone. Each of us connects differently, and as such we all have a different spiritual mission in this world, distinct from all others. We know this to be true simply because we are all here.

Judaism teaches that nothing exists in the world that is extra or superfluous. God, the perfect Being, creates everything and everyone for a precise reason with a distinct purpose and mission that no one else can carry out. Everything and everyone happens for a reason.

Each of us has a purpose and Judaism teaches us to live in such a way as to reflect this belief. We treat rich or famous people as though *they* somehow possess a more important mission than the rest of the world. But just because more people are aware of someone's existence or of his or her accomplishments does not in any way imply that role is more significant. This critical idea plays out in both our professional and spiritual lives. The CEO of any company will of course be more well-known (and certainly better paid) than someone lower on the corporate ladder, but, by definition, if someone occupies a position in a company, *any* position really, that means he or she is necessary for the company's success. I am not suggesting that knowing this will necessarily translate into greater job satisfaction, but it *should* translate into a greater sense of worth, that one is necessary and critical for the successful functioning of that company.

This applies equally to the CEO and the person who cleans the office at night. The roles are different, but both are necessary and important. One of my favorite people with whom I had the privilege of working was MJE's maintenance man, Lester. Lester took great pride in everything he did. From the meticulous way in which he would set up the chairs and tables for our services and classes to the rigorous cleaning he would give our offices, you could see how much pride Lester took in his work. He knew how important it was for MJE's event center to look great—how significant first impressions are—and so he put his all into everything he did. As I'd be preparing my sermons every Friday, I would see Lester arranging the chairs and moving the tables. Although our roles were very different, both truly had value.

This applies equally to the spiritual realm, although in a different way. Americans tend to look at rabbis as the "holy" people in the community, the ones with all the Jewish knowledge, who observe all the mitzvot and the only ones who can perform Jewish ceremonies and rituals. Nothing could be farther from the truth. Jewish scholarship and leadership were never supposed to be concentrated in the hands of an elite few. Just the opposite: every Jew, regardless of his or her background, was meant to observe the laws of the Torah and become a scholar. Just as the Torah was revealed at Sinai to *every* member of the community, and not to just the rabbis and scholars, Jewish learning and observance is for everyone and anyone who truly desires it. A rabbi is usually more learned than the typical layman because he has spent more time studying, but ultimately, he is just a teacher. That is what the word "rabbi" or "rav" simply means, a teacher. He teaches and helps inspire the community, but that is not to somehow imply he is the *only* one who possesses Jewish wisdom and knowledge, or the only one committed to observing the mitzvot. The gap that exists in other religions between religious leaders and layman was never supposed to exist in Judaism. That is why many Jewish people, who are *not* rabbis, make sure to study Torah on a regular basis, pray three times a day, and can truly be called "Torah scholars," although they are not technically rabbis. They may be lawyers, doctors, or therapists, but since they devote time to studying Jewish texts and are serious about their religious observances, there isn't this gap between the Jewish layman and the "rabbi," as we often find in other faith systems. I think of this when I'm traveling on the Long Island Railroad and I see groups of professionals on their way to work studying Talmud or other Judaic texts. It's inspiring to see because these individuals do not simply see their rabbi or religious leader as the only ones on a spiritual journey. They are chartering their own spiritual path and growing their own relationship with God, becoming as learned and knowledgeable as they can. I also think about this when I'm praying at the MJE Shabbat service and one of the participants from the service gets up to share a short sermon on the weekly Torah portion. It was important to impress upon my students that it's not just the rabbi who can share words of Torah, but that it's incumbent upon all of us to study and inspire others with words of wisdom from our tradition.

How important is it for us to grow *ourselves* spiritually, or have we fallen into the common misperception that this is only for rabbis and religious leaders? How seriously do we take study and religious observance for ourselves or have we relegated those activities to the "spiritual elite?" There really is no such thing since each of us was created with a mission of our own, a mission for both the material and spiritual parts of our lives. If we fail to cultivate the spiritual aspect of who we are, then that spiritual connection becomes lost from the world, since it was unique to us and us alone.

I once invited someone to come to MJE's weeknight classes. The man, named David, responded, "Rabbi, I'm sorry, but I didn't even go to Hebrew School." I replied, "David, it isn't an advanced Talmud class, it's a basic Judaism course. You're a smart guy, I guarantee you'll understand everything." Someone else I was encouraging to learn to read Hebrew said to me, "Rabbi, I'm already thirty-two, if I haven't learned it by now then it's not gonna happen." I said, "Wow, I never knew there was a cut-off age for learning Hebrew or getting more involved in studying the Torah. The greatest Talmudic sage, Rabbi Akiva, was forty when he began!" More importantly though, I shared how important it was for him to find and ultimately fulfill his own personal spiritual mission.

Our unique mission in this world, both in the material and spiritual parts of our lives, is a gift from our Creator that we can choose to cultivate, or simply ignore. Following that mission, wherever it takes us, gives purpose and meaning to everything we do.

Notes

1. Karl Moore, "The Parachute Packer—the Best Story I Have Ever Heard," *Forbes*, July 18, 2012, https://www.forbes.com/sites/karlmoore/2012/07/18/the-parachute-packer-the-best-story-i-have-ever-heard/#27efac83d8b6; https://www.youtube.com/watch?v=JqtUlMA3Jqo&t=6s.
2. Ronald Fischer, PhD, and Diana Boer, PhD, "What Is More Important for National Well-Being: Money or Autonomy? A Meta-Analysis of Well-Being, Burnout and Anxiety Across 63 Societies," *Journal of Personality and Social Psychology*, Vol. 101, Issue 1.

3. Samuel 1, Chapter 20.
4. Talmud, Bava Batra 10b.
5. Commentary of the Ohr Hachayim on Deuteronomy on 22:1–3.

Chapter 8
ETHICS VS. ETIQUETTE

Eighth Commandment: *Thou Shalt Choose Right Over Like*

One of the personal issues I struggle with is my need for approval. I spend time and energy trying to get people to like me: friends, colleagues, students, donors, even my wife and children. Of course, it would be difficult to be a successful rabbi, fund-raiser, husband, or father if people didn't like me, but it goes deeper than this. In more recent years I found a friend which has made it even easier to be "liked": Facebook. I came a little late to the Facebook party, but in a pretty short period of time I accumulated close to four thousand "friends," and my posts can get hundreds—sometimes even thousands—of people to "like" me!

For me, Facebook is like a drug to an addict because, although it feels good to be liked, ultimately it doesn't make me any happier. My feelings were confirmed by a study conducted by the University of Michigan, which concluded that increased Facebook use drives people's levels of happiness down and increases feelings of loneliness and isolation. Like any addiction, we get a quick high, which keeps us coming back for more "liking" and more approval from other people.[1]

Why do we seek approval from others and why is it so important what others think of us?

Every summer I have the privilege of leading the MJE trip to Israel, and a few summers ago I did so in the middle of Israel's war in Gaza. The trip was nonetheless awesome. Aside from being inspired by Israel's incredible fortitude in the face of daily rocket attacks from terror groups, I came away with the following conclusion: Israelis don't care nearly as much as we Americans do about what other people say or think. I'm not saying they don't care at all. No one likes to be criticized, but from the attitudes of the soldiers and others we met that summer and the many others I have met over the years, I have concluded that Israelis draw their attitude, not from what other people think, but from what they believe is right.

Choosing "right" over "like" is reflected in a compelling teaching of the Torah: the book of Genesis tells us that after the flood God sent to destroy the world, Noah planted a vineyard and became intoxicated. The Torah describes a very unflattering scene where Noah is found drunk and disrobed in his tent.[2] The reactions of Noah's three sons, Shem, Cham, and Yefet, to their father in this state were different, and according to the Jewish Sages, laid the groundwork for future generations.

Cham gazed at his father, and, as the commentaries explain, he took advantage of his father's compromised state and violated him. However, Noah's other sons, Shem and Yefet, took a garment, walked backwards so as not to show him any disrespect, and covered their father's nakedness with the cloth.

In describing this act of respect, the Torah says, "and Shem and Yefet took," but the word "took" is written in the singular even though it was *both* Shem and Yefet who covered Noah.[3] Rashi, the biblical commentator, tells us that Shem initiated the action and Yefet followed him, and therefore: "Shem merited the mitzvah of tzitzit and Yefet merited the mitzvah of burial." Just a few verses later, the Torah tells us that Noah blesses his son, Yefet, by saying that God should "grant beauty to Yefet"[4] and we have a tradition that whereas the Jewish people come from Shem, Greek civilization is descended from Yefet.

What does this all mean?

Rabbi Joseph B. Soloveitchick speaks about two different motivating factors in human behavior, Etiquette and Ethics: "Ethics obligates a person to do what is right and just, even if he is by himself and there are no other people around who will see him to praise his actions. To the contrary, even if there are other people there who will mock him for his desire to do what is right, he will do what is right because of his strong sense of ethic. Etiquette, on the other hand, is a matter of beauty which is dependent upon the input and the approval of other people. Etiquette changes from time to time and from country to country. Etiquette is something that emerges from the way in which something will appear in the eyes of other people."[5]

Shem, explains Rabbi Soloveitchik, had the courage to be the first to cover his father, even though no one was telling him to do so because he understood from his sense of ethics that covering his father was the right thing to do. And that's why the Jewish people, the descendants of Shem, merited the mitzvah of *tzitzit*. *Tzitzit* are ritual fringes worn beneath one's clothing, and so they reflect an *inner* sense of right and wrong, regardless of what appears on the outside or what others may say.

Yefet, on the other hand, did not act because it was the right thing to do. He covered his father only *after* Shem did. And he did so, says the Rabbi Soloveitchick, "only so that Shem would look upon him with a good eye . . . It was only then that he helped, because at this point it was not only a matter of 'ethics,' it was a matter of 'etiquette'."[6]

Therefore, the reward for Yefet was burial because the whole idea of burying someone after they have passed away stems from the honor we give to the deceased: it just doesn't *look* right to casually discard the remains of a person after their soul has departed. Burial is the ultimate expression of etiquette; the blessing Noah gave to Yefet who did the right thing, but only did so to look good.

Ultimately the Divine Presence rests in the tents of Shem and not Yefet because, for God to be with us, for the Almighty to dwell in our midst, our actions need to be motivated more by ethics than etiquette.

We must make decisions in life which are based on what's ultimately right, and not merely by what will bring us greater approval. In some situations, we are forced to choose: during the war in Gaza in 2014, Israel was forced to choose between acting in a way that was moral or in a manner that would gain the world's approval. To receive the world's blessing during the war in Gaza would have meant Israel giving up its moral imperative to self-defense and keeping its people in harm's way. On the intellectual level, most people agreed Israel was justified in doing whatever was necessary to stop the rocket attacks, but Israel still *looked* bad because innocent children were tragically being killed. The terror group Hamas was launching rockets from hospitals, homes, and mosques so that when Israel retaliated, it looked like a monster. But deciding *not* to retaliate and destroy those rocket installations, which were causing severe harm and damage to Israel and her people, because it would bring world condemnation, would have been choosing etiquette over ethics.

Israelis, in general, are more concerned with ethics than they are with etiquette. You will probably never hear an Israeli say "excuse me" when he or she bumps into you on a public bus, but only in Israel will you see the bus driver put the bus in park and get up to help a mother with her baby carriage onto the bus. He may look and sound gruff and uncaring, but ultimately, he does the right thing.

We need to stop caring so much about what others think and be more concerned with what's right. Sometimes the right thing isn't always the popular thing: saying no to a night out with friends when you have a family obligation certainly won't make you more popular with your friends, but it's the right thing to do. Not participating in some gossip about a co-worker may cost you some status points in the office, but it too is an expression of ethics over etiquette.

Politics and Popularity

When it comes to politics, we have become accustomed to our elected officials choosing policies based on popularity over the greater good and what is in the best interests of their constituency. However, there are many examples of leaders who choose ethics over personal gain. Take for example Governor Dannel Malloy, who began his second term as governor of Connecticut in January 2015. In the fall of 2015, Islamic extremists carried out a series of coordinated, violent terrorist attacks in Paris. The attacks inflamed public fears of terrorism in the United States and sparked a wave of anti-refugee proposals by local, state, and national politicians. More than half of the nation's governors declared that, regardless of any increased security vetting, Syrian refugees would not be welcomed in their states. Just three days after the Paris attacks, Malloy called for federal authorities to apply rigorous screening methods, but also declared that Connecticut would continue to accept refugees from Syria. Two days later, he personally welcomed a family of Syrian refugees to New Haven after the governor of Indiana turned them away.

Elizabeth Redenbaugh was sworn in as a member of North Carolina's New Hanover County school board in December 2008. A few months after she was elected, the school board proposed a redistricting plan that appeared likely to result in increased socioeconomic and racial segregation in Wilmington middle schools. Supporters of the measure asserted that desegregation via busing just had not worked. Redenbaugh wrote an op-ed in which she pointed out that the proposed "neighborhood schools" map would concentrate poor and overwhelmingly black children in several schools, and that she "could not in good conscience send any child from any background to a school" that data suggested was likely to fail. Wilmington parents were bitterly divided over the plan. In early 2010, after a contentious community debate, the school board voted 4–3 to approve the new map. Redenbaugh was the only Republican and the only white member of the school board to vote against the plan. In the ensuing weeks, parents bombarded the school board with complaints about last-minute provisions that had not been publicly debated. The school board reopened discussions over a slightly revised middle school map, but after a second heated debate, the board approved the revised map by the same 4–3 margin. Once again,

Elizabeth Redenbaugh was the only Republican and only white school board member to dissent.

In October 2010, the state of North Carolina asked New Hanover County to sign an affidavit certifying that it was not intentionally segregating county schools based on race or socioeconomic status. Redenbaugh opposed the school board's decision to endorse the affidavit. The board approved the certification anyway, saying that if indeed segregation happened, it was unintentional. Elizabeth Redenbaugh was not re-elected to the New Hanover County school board in 2012 but remains an active and positive member of her community.[7]

Staying committed to certain principles may not get you reelected, but it will help you to live a life of purpose and meaning. Popularity may earn you some points in the short term, but to live *beyond the instant* you must have a set of principles to which you remain committed. This applies equally to our spiritual lives. If, for example, you observe certain dietary restrictions, choosing a restaurant should reflect that. Asking one's work colleagues to hold a lunch meeting at a kosher restaurant may not earn you more popularity, but if that's what you're committed to, then it's the *right* thing to ask.

Popularity and Plastic

There's a true story of a luncheon with prominent lawyers in London who had as their guest speaker none other than Charles, Prince of Wales. One of the lawyers who attended the luncheon was an observant Jew who ordered a kosher meal. Some of you may know that the kosher meals in these circumstances come double-wrapped in plastic with cutlery that usually breaks when you use it. It can sometimes look a bit messy. As the lawyer was eating his kosher meal another attorney walked by and asked him, "Why do you have to make such a spectacle of yourself? I'm also Jewish, you know, why not just eat whatever everyone else is eating?"

Later, after Prince Charles finished his presentation and was making his way out of the room, he passed by the table of the observant Jew and took notice of all the plastic. He stopped at the table and asked him why he was eating something different from the rest of the crowd. The lawyer explained that he observed the Jewish laws of *kashrut*. In reply, Prince Charles shared how, as part of his university studies, he attended a theological seminary where they studied the Jewish dietary laws. The two then got into a whole conversation about diet and spirituality. When the other Jewish man overheard the conversation, he walked over and chimed in, "You know, I'm also Jewish." Prince Charles turned to the man and asked, "So where is your kosher meal?"

The kosher man chose ethics over etiquette. He put up with a little plastic and flimsy cutlery to follow something in which he believed. When you're gaining other people's approval, etiquette may win the day, but to earn respect you need ethics. Having other people approve our actions may make us feel better in the short term, but we can only attain lasting happiness and set an example for others when we know we're doing the right thing. Legendary Hall of Fame pitcher Sandy Koufax refused to pitch in the first game of the 1965 World Series because it fell on Yom Kippur. That decision inspired not only Jewish people to take greater pride in their religious beliefs, but it influenced other athletes and people everywhere to make decisions based on principle and not popularity. (It probably didn't hurt that Koufax's team, the Los Angeles Dodgers, went on to win the series, with Koufax being named the series MVP!)

Looking Up and Not Around

What motivates our actions and behavior? Do we act out of a real ethical standard or do we simply copy what other people do so we can please our family, friends, or colleagues? By following a moral system that is above and beyond a humanely-devised one, we can know we are developing a path that reflects a genuine ethic and not simply following what is politically correct or what everyone else does.

When making important life decisions, we should be looking up and not around. Those choices may not always get us more "likes," but if they are informed by something above, by a Force greater and wiser than ourselves, they will no doubt bring us greater meaning and fulfillment, and help us look *beyond the instant.*

Notes

1.	Diane Swanbrow, "Facebook use predicts declines in happiness, new study finds," *Michigan News*, University of Michigan, August 14, 2013, http://www.ns.umich .edu/new/releases/21626-facebook-use-predicts-declines-in-happiness-new -study-finds.
2.	Genesis 9:21.
3.	Genesis 9:23.
4.	Genesis 9:27.
5.	Rabbi Hershel Schachter, *Nefesh Harav* (New York: 1994), 272–273.
6.	Ibid.
7.	Elizabeth Redenbaugh won the 2011 JFK Profile in Courage Award. John F. Kennedy Presidential Library and Museum: https://www.jfklibrary.org/Events -and-Awards/Profile-in-Courage-Award/Award-Recipients/Elizabeth-Redenbaugh -2011.aspx.

Chapter 9
CELEBRATING THE JOURNEY

Ninth Commandment: *Thou Shalt be Present and Aware*

Ever since I can remember, I've been obsessed with results. To this day, I have a difficult time enjoying the process necessary to produce end results, even when I like the activity involved. One example is speech writing. Although I love doing research and learning new things, the knowledge that by the end of the week I need to have a polished sermon prepared for my congregation robs me of much of the fun involved in speech writing. You'd think that after twenty years of speech making I'd be better able to enjoy the learning process, but the obsession with producing the best result takes over.

What is more important in life? Achieving our goals or enjoying the experience we go through to get there? Most of our time in this world is spent on the process and not on that moment of glory when we've reached our destination, and yet that whole experience is viewed merely as a necessary mean to accomplish the end goal. What's more important?

Adam and Eve were placed in the beautiful Garden of Eden and allowed to eat from any of the fruit-bearing trees except the Tree of Knowledge. The cunning snake managed to convince Eve to eat from the Tree of Knowledge and then Eve, in turn, gives some of its fruit to Adam. Adam, Eve, and the snake were all punished for their disobedience and strangely enough, so was the ground: " . . . cursed is the ground because of you."[1] Why is the ground cursed? There are three players here: Adam, Eve, and the snake. What did the ground do? Why is it also being punished?

The great sixteenth century Kabbalist, Rabbi Isaac Luria, explained that the ground sinned in that it produced trees that didn't taste like the fruit they were bearing. The Torah tells us that on the third day of creation God commanded the earth to sprout forth fruit trees: "fruit trees which produce fruit according to their own species."[2] Rashi, the biblical commentator, writes that this means that the ground was supposed to produce trees that tasted like the fruit they bear. The trees themselves, all throughout the Garden of Eden, were supposed have a sweet taste just like the fruit they produced. However, the ground didn't comply with this command, and with the exception of the Tree of Knowledge, none of the trees themselves had a sweet taste, just the fruit they produced.

But what is the significance of trees that are supposed to taste like their fruit?

The Sin of the Ground and the Lie of the Snake

The great sage and mystic Rabbi Abraham Isaac Kook explained that both the sin of the ground and the lie of the snake were their attempts at convincing man that they were created and placed in this world only for the product, just for the fruit. The earth was commanded to produce trees that also had a sweet taste to convey the important teaching that in life the process and the journey are also supposed to be sweet, not just the result—not only the fruit. The tree represents what we go through in life to produce the kinds of things we want in the end. Ultimately what's valuable is not only the result, not just the fruit, but also the tree. The journey and the process we go through to get there is just as important.

Rabbi David Aaron, an inspirational author and teacher, compares this to someone trying to climb Mount Everest. The goal of the mountain climber is, of course, to make it to the top and to plant a flag to indicate he or she has made it. On the way up, during the grueling and arduous climb, the climber gets a call on his radio letting him know there's a helicopter in the near vicinity that is available to take him to the top in a matter of seconds. The man declines the offer on his radio. Why? Why does he turn the helicopter offer down and instead put himself through the extreme physical challenge of continuing to climb on his own? Because it's not just about getting to the top—the climb itself has value.

There's a fascinating rabbinic passage that teaches that during the nine months of pregnancy an angel teaches the child in utero all the wisdom of the Torah from beginning to end.[3] However, right before the mother is about to give birth and the child emerges, the Talmud tells us that the angel gives a little flick on the child's lip, causing it to forget all the wisdom it had learned during the pregnancy. Why does the angel do this? Why not let the child come into this world as a wise sage? Because immersion in Torah study is also a value in and of itself. Having the experience of studying and learning wisdom is one of our cherished values—it's not just about being the great scholar, but it's also about the journey, the opportunity to be involved in the process of learning. That too is supposed to be sweet.

Most of us were not taught to think in this way. We live in a goal-oriented society which centers around achieving results, particularly at work. Our bosses want to see results. They want to see the finished product on their desk by nine the next morning, and they don't care about the journey or the kind of experience we may have had in producing the work—*just make sure it's on my desk first thing in the morning.* That mentality, which may be important in what we do professionally, seeps into our consciousness and influences the way we look at everything in life. It can result in severe repercussions that ultimately discourage us from pursuing some of the most beautiful things in life. Take art as one example: Perhaps you're interested in doing some painting, but after visiting a museum and seeing paintings by great artists like Rembrandt, Van Gogh, and Monet, you realize you'll never produce anything like these masters and so you don't bother trying. But who said your result needed to be on the level of Van Gogh to matter? Who said it needs to come out looking like this or that? Doesn't the *experience* of painting in and of itself have value? Perhaps painting reveals some artistic side that needs to be expressed, or it relaxes you in some way.

The same applies in the realm of spirituality. I had a student without much of a background in Judaism, but who started coming to MJE to learn more about his heritage. After some studying, he began to observe a few Jewish traditions which he said spoke to him and which he enjoyed practicing. However, one day at services he saw someone wearing a large yarmulke, swaying back and forth and praying fervently from a Hebrew prayer book, and he got turned off. He stopped attending our classes and services, and when I asked him why he stopped coming, he answered that he could never imagine himself ending up like that other person, praying so fervently and being so meticulous in his religious observance. "What's the point?" he asked. "If I'm not interested in ending up like that guy, why bother?"

In classic rabbinic form, I answered his question with my own question: "Who said it's all about how you end up?" I asked him. "If you're enjoying observing the traditions you are engaged with now, then what does it matter what might happen down the road?" In Judaism, the experience and process we go through, as well as the effort we put in, matters at least as much as where we end up. We need not worry *where* on the religious spectrum we end up as much as *how much of ourselves* we are investing right now. What effort are we putting into our spiritual and religious growth?

In the Ethics of Our Fathers,* the Jewish Sages declared, "It is not for you to finish the job but you are not free to withdraw from it altogether."[4] Failing to reach the summit of the mountain is acceptable, but

---

* Ethical teachings of the Jewish Sages found in the Mishna, the first part of the Oral Tradition recorded.

failing to try is not. The Sages continue: "If you studied much Torah you will receive great reward." Notice the language—"if you studied much Torah"—if you engage in the experience of developing your spiritual knowledge base, you will receive great reward. They do not say "if you become a great scholar" you will receive great reward because the reward is not for the knowledge acquired but for the effort put in. As another from the Ethics of our Fathers explicitly states: "According to the effort is the reward."[5] The end goal, here the level of scholarship, is not ultimately what serves as our greatest reward, but rather the effort we put in and the experience we go through in trying to reach our goals in life.

At the completion of a tractate (section) of Talmud there is a celebration called a *siyum* at which the following prayer is recited: "They toil (i.e. those who extend effort to study Torah) and we toil (those who work as artisans), we toil and receive reward and they toil and *don't* receive reward." Is it true that only those who toil and work hard studying Torah receive reward? Don't those who work as artisans and other forms of business also receive reward for their hard work?

The great nineteenth-century sage, Rabbi Israel Meir Kagan, commonly referred to as the Chafetz Chaim, answered that both the student of Torah and the artisan receive reward, but only the one studying Torah receives reward for the *effort*. The artisan on the other hand gets rewarded only for what he or she produces. The artisan may extend enormous effort to produce a certain vase for example, putting in many extra hours of work. However, at the end of the day, he or she gets paid only what the market says the vase is worth. Nothing more, nothing less. Not so with Torah study. When it comes to Torah study and one's spiritual pursuits, one receives reward not simply for whatever results are attained, but also for the effort one invests.

A Party for One Page

There's a true story of a gentleman from Europe who was never taught much about Judaism as a child. He came to the United States and one of his children, despite having no Jewish education, began to gravitate to Jewish life and to Torah study. The son eventually became religiously observant and quite Jewishly knowledgeable. As his son's connection to Torah developed, the father's curiosity was aroused and on occasion the father would ask his son to study with him. He was particularly fascinated by Talmud and so the father asked his son to teach him Talmud. At first the son was reluctant. "Look, Dad," the son said to his father, "the ideas in the Talmud can get very complicated and the language (Aramaic) is very difficult." But the father was persistent and eventually he got his son to study with him. They studied Talmud diligently every day and after an entire year they managed to finish one page. Although it was only one page, the father was very proud of this accomplishment and asked his son if they could celebrate with a *siyum,* a religious celebration. However, a *siyum* is usually made when one finishes an *entire* tractate of Talmud, not just one page. Undeterred, the father called a rabbi and was somehow put in touch with the late Rabbi Moshe Feinstein, one of the greatest Talmudic masters of his generation and a saintly figure. When Rav Moshe (as people affectionately referred to him) heard the question and the whole story he was inspired and he answered the father: "You may certainly make a *siyum* on one page of the Talmud, but on one condition: you let me join the celebration. This is an extraordinary accomplishment and I want to be a part of it." The father threw a festive siyum and the great Rav Moshe attended.

A party for one page of Talmud. Why? Because we should not only celebrate results or when we reach our destination, but also the journey and the investment we make. Remember it's not just the fruit produced, it's also about the tree—the experience we have in getting there. We must learn to celebrate and find happiness not only when we reach our goals, but also in the many moments along the way.

But this is easier said than done. In a world hung up on results and in which technology increasingly keeps us from being in the moment, how can we better enjoy the journey and savor the experience? We need to train ourselves to be more present. Jewish tradition offers different practices, which if studied and applied consistently, help us become more mindful and present. The ones which stand out are the Sabbath and Blessings.

The Sabbath: Blocking Out Distractions

The Bible commands the Jewish people to observe the Sabbath by refraining from doing "work" on the seventh day of each week. The biblical term "work" is understood in the Talmud not as the exertion of physical labor like we usually think of the term, but rather the thirty-nine activities that went into the building and maintenance of the ancient Tabernacle (the portable sanctuary with which the Israelites traveled in the wilderness). Each of those activities involve the creative use of our intelligence and skill to manipulate the physical world in one way or another. In modern times those activities translate into abstaining from driving in a car or using a telephone or smart phone, since the electricity which powers them falls under one or more of these thirty-nine acts of "work." By refraining from those creative activities one day each week we turn the world back over to God, declaring the Almighty as the ultimate source of creation. Besides making that theological statement, refraining from engaging in these creative activities also forces us to temporarily shut out many of life's distractions so we can properly focus on what is truly important in life: our families, our community, and our spiritual relationship with God.

The Sabbath of course contains positive activities such as lighting candles, reciting the Kiddush, eating three meals, and praying in synagogue. But it's the refraining from these thirty-nine creative activities (and their derivatives) which enables us to use those positive commandments to connect with our family, community, and God in a more profound and deeper way than we otherwise could with all the distractions. The following story which I heard in a speech from author and radio host Marianne Williamson makes the point quite powerfully: One evening Marianne was sitting in her home at her computer answering some emails. Beside her was Marianne's eight-year-old daughter playing a video game on her computer. In the background, some music was on that Marianne was listening to, and the TV was playing a movie which her daughter looked up from her video game to glance at occasionally. Lots of stimulation! Outside a thunderstorm was raging, and then suddenly everything went black. The electricity in Marianne's home went out as a blackout descended on their Detroit suburb. The computers both mother and daughter were using shut down as did the music and TV and of course, all the lights.

At first Marianne's daughter became frightened, until they found some candles and lit them. There was nothing else to do so they began to talk: five minutes, ten minutes, twenty minutes flew by as mother and daughter chatted by the small candle that provided only a little light. Then just as quickly as everything had shut down, everything went back on! The lights, computers, music, and TV all suddenly came to life as the electricity was restored. Marianne got back to her emails and her daughter resumed her video game playing as though nothing had happened.

About five minutes later, Marianne's daughter turned to her mother and said, "Mommy, do you think we'll ever get that chance again?"

"What chance?" her mother asked.

"The chance to talk like that," her daughter answered. "I don't remember ever speaking with you like that. There's always something else going on."

An eight-year-old felt the special bond that was forged in those few minutes. She could feel the difference between a conversation with distractions and one where there was focus. An eight-year-old, and really, all of us, know when we're truly connecting with someone and how challenging that can be when we are so bombarded by technology—by things that are supposed to be making our lives easier. We live in such a distracting world. That's why we all need some form of Shabbat in our lives, a kind of blackout to ensure we truly connect with each other, our community, and our spiritual source. We can't rely on our electricity going out to ensure we have some real quality time with each other and that our lives are infused with purpose and meaning. This is why, out of all of the Torah's observances to which I have found young people attracted to today, it is hands down the Sabbath. People understand that technology, while an indispensable tool for virtually every profession and trade today, is also keeping us from deepening our relationships and finding more value and ultimately happiness in life. Hence the new "unplugged weekend retreats" that have become so popular. These digital detoxing weekends, which first became popular in the United States and then found their way to Europe and Australia, stress mindfulness and begin by having everyone drop their smart phones into a box or bag.

Our shared crisis in digital distraction requires far more than just a weekend of change. From grade school to adulthood, our device addictions eat away at our downtime and capacity for reflection and creativity. Research and reporting continue to underscore the mental and emotional value of doing nothing—being alone with our thoughts, meditating, praying, or reading. One series of studies found that people put in a quiet room for six to fifteen minutes and asked to think quietly couldn't bear it and chose to give themselves a shock to escape their boredom. National Public Radio's story on the study summarized it this way: "Stripped of their books, cellphones and other distractions, many, including a majority of men, preferred to instead pass the time by reaching for the sole form of electronic entertainment in the room: a nine-volt battery administering a 'severe static shock' when touched."

"It's probably an issue of how we can control our minds and thoughts," Timothy Wilson, professor of psychology at the University of Virginia and a co-author of the study, said. The study attempted to measure the enjoyment found in allowing people's minds to wander. According to NPR, "That represents a novel approach to the study of human distractibility, in which the 'wandering mind' is often itself the distraction: a symptom of our multitasking, digitized culture that interrupts our pleasure reading, test-taking and work lives . . . Wilson says he and his colleagues were initially skeptical of including the shock device as an outlet for subjects to escape their thoughts. Given that participants were warned the contraption would give them a painful jolt, the researchers asked the seemingly obvious: 'Why is someone going to shock themselves?' The most common answers: boredom and curiosity."[6]

As this study shows, we're distracting ourselves to death.

Our world is in desperate need of Shabbat, especially as the number of times we look at our smart phones each day continues to rise (in 2014, it was every six minutes or at least 150 times per day). FOMO (Fear of Missing Out) is also wreaking havoc with teenagers glued to their smart phones lest they miss out on "something else" going on. Shabbat helps train us to be present in the here and now so we can enjoy the moment without having to think about what else we *could* be doing. For that, we need the thirty-nine acts of work from which we refrain, or some form of artificial restriction to which we adhere, if we are to learn how to enjoy the journey and savor the moment.

Blessings and the Power of Gratitude

Another device designed to help us become more present and aware are the blessings the Jewish sages ordained to be said before eating. Referred to as "birchot hanehenim" or blessings over pleasure, the sages ordained different blessings (depending on what one is consuming) to be said immediately before eating. Before eating fruit, for example, the blessing of "God who creates fruit of the trees" is said, or before eating a vegetable we recite, "God who creates the fruit of the ground." The reason we recite these blessings is not to bless God (since we do not believe the Almighty *needs* our blessing), but rather to verbally acknowledge the source of food in the physical world, God. The Hebrew word for blessing, *bracha*, is linguistically related to the Hebrew word *beraicha*, which means spring. Just as a spring serves as a source of water, by saying a blessing we acknowledge God as the *source* of whatever physical pleasure we are about to enjoy. This practice is critical in developing a true awareness and appreciation for the blessings in life we take for granted. This is precisely why there is also a Jewish practice to recite a blessing after we come out of the bathroom. Although it seems strange to says a blessing over the discharge of bodily waste, by verbally acknowledging how parts of our body are working properly we make ourselves aware of something wonderful we know is happening, but of which we are not conscious and therefore usually take for granted.

Generally, we only appreciate the basic gifts of life when they're threatened. As long as everything is working, we go about our business and see things like having to go to the bathroom as a nuisance. This reminds me of a time years ago when I had to undergo a hernia operation. Thankfully the surgery went well, but the surgeon wouldn't release me from the hospital until I moved my bowels. When I was finally able to I began to appreciate my digestive system more than ever before. I remember how for the next few weeks going to the bathroom made me happy to be alive. But a month later that awareness and appreciation came to an end. I became conditioned to going to the bathroom and once again took my bodily workings for granted, except when I thought about the words I was saying in the post-bathroom blessing. Reciting that blessing enabled me to properly appreciate my body even when it was, thank God, not threatened and working well. This is the net effect of reciting blessings: to become aware and ultimately grateful for something positive in our lives which we previously ignored.

The more aware we become of those blessings we *already* have, be it food or the health of our bodies, the happier those blessings can make us. When we are not conscious of them, we become needy for things we don't have and are unable to be grateful for what we do have; as a result, we're less happy. Studies demonstrate that grateful people, namely those appreciative of the blessings they already possess, are more content people. Robert Emmons, a professor of psychology at University of California at Davis, is the founder and editor-in-chief of *The Journal of Positive Psychology* and author of the books *Gratitude Works!: A 21-Day Program for Creating Emotional Prosperity* and *Thanks! How the New Science of Gratitude Can Make You Happier.* Emmons's studies find that gratitude lowers blood pressure, improves immune function, and facilitates more efficient sleep. Gratitude is also associated with lifestyle changes including exercise, improvements in nutrition and diet, being less likely to smoke and abuse alcohol, and taking medications appropriately. "Gratitude blocks toxic emotions, such as envy, resentment, regret, and depression, which can destroy our happiness," Emmons said.[7]

Gratitude also plays a role in overcoming traumatic stress disorder. A 2006 study published in *Behavior Research and Therapy* found that Vietnam War veterans who felt and expressed gratitude regularly correlated with lower levels of PTSD. The study also found that gratitude correlated with a range of well-being factors for veterans.[8]

Uttering a few simple words over a piece of fruit (or any food item) makes us aware of the beautiful part of our reality we otherwise neglect. Finding joy in the blessings *we already have* is imperative to enjoying the journey—it allows us to appreciate what we have in our lives right now and to focus less on what we might receive when we reach the desired destination. The more appreciative we become of what we have right before us today, the more we will savor the moments and experiences of our daily lives, and the less we will rely on reaching goals to find happiness.

For those who tend to live from high to high and who only find fulfillment in reaching goals, reciting blessings is a vital practice which can help savor the wonderful experiences along the way. As John Lennon wrote in "Beautiful Boy (Darling Boy)," one of his post-Beatles songs, "Life is what happens to you while you're busy making other plans." If we can't find joy in the everyday, in the process necessary to make our dreams a reality, then our reality will be a dreary one. We will end up placing way too much pressure on ourselves to achieve our goals, since too much of our happiness is wrapped up in reaching them. We risk becoming like those who "live for the weekends" but who are unhappy during the week, which comprises the bulk of our lives!

Besides, reaching our goals becomes less realistic when we don't find joy or value in the journey along the way. Few of us have the discipline to remain committed to something we find uninspiring. This principle applies well to our spiritual growth. We all need goals and should delight in reaching them, but as I always tell my students, we need to find the fun and sweetness in the journey.

We also need to recognize that the journey is going to be radically different for each of us. If you've gotten into the bad habit of routinely speaking ill of colleagues and friends, then doing so *less often* will be your spiritual journey. If another person reached their goal of restraining themselves from speaking what Jewish tradition calls "lashon hara" (literally *bad speech*), then that person's journey will be to try to hold back even more and get to a place where refraining becomes easier. Referring to the Sabbath, which we discussed earlier, if one never lit Shabbat candles* or recited the Kiddush** to usher in the Shabbat on Friday nights, then doing so is a wonderful journey to begin and a great step forward. If Shabbat candle lighting and Kiddush are already givens in another person's religious life, then the next step in that person's journey might be attending Shabbat prayer services, and if one already does this, then making it on time could be the next step! Similarly, if one has never given charity, then doing so on whatever level is a step forward. If one has given some charity but done so minimally or not regularly, then giving on a regular basis, increasing the amount or aspiring to the Jewish ideal of tithing one's net income (trying to give 10 percent of one's annual earnings, after taxes), would be the next journey in one's spiritual life. Whatever the example, the journey is unique to each person and it's imperative to find the joy and sweetness in the experience itself, not just when we achieve the goals. The tree must also be sweet, not just the fruits we produce.

If we can find joy in the journey, we will not only find greater joy in the everyday but ironically, we will also increase the likelihood of reaching the goal. Zev Vilne, who is a member of Knesset, Israel's parliament, is head of tourism in Israel. He was meeting with one of Israel's top tour

---

* Candles which are lit before the Sabbath to create an aura of joy and peace.

** A prayer recited over wine on the Sabbath to recognize the sanctity and special nature of the day within the home.

guides who had this extraordinary reputation of *always* being able to make to it to the top of Mount Hermon (Israel's highest mountain) with his tour groups. Zev, the member of Knesset, asked the tour guide how he was always able to accomplish this with all his groups. "I heard most other tour guides never make it to the top; what's your secret?" he asked the tour guide. The guide responded, "When the other guides are leading their groups and they begin to get tired, they usually have them stop and look forward to see the top of the mountain, but when my group begins to get tired I do just the opposite. I tell them to turn around and look back to see how far they've already come."

Turn around and look back, see how far you've come. Take pride in what you've accomplished and enjoy the journey.

Notes

1. Genesis 3:17.
2. Genesis 1:11.
3. Talmud, Nidah 30b.
4. Ethics of Our Fathers 2:16.
5. Ethics of Our Fathers 5:23.
6. Gregory Barber, "Surrounded by Digital Distractions, We Can't Even Stop to Think," National Public Radio. July 3, 2014. https://www.npr.org/sections/alltechconsidered/2014/07/03/328137640/surrounded-by-digital-distractions-we-cant-even-stop-to-think.
7. Robert Emmons, "Gratitude Is Good Medicine," *UC Davis Medical Center.* http://www.ucdmc.ucdavis.edu/medicalcenter/features/2015–2016/11/20151125_gratitude.html.
8. Kashdan, Uswatte, Julian, "Gratitude and Hedonic and Eudaimonic Well-Being in Vietnam War Veterans," *Behavior Research and Therapy*, Volume 44, Issue 2, February 2006, 177–199; Amy Morin, "7 Scientifically Proven Benefits of Gratitude," *Psychology Today*, April 2017, psychologytoday.com/blog/what-mentally-strong-people-dont-do/201504/7-scientifically-proven-benefits-gratitude.

Chapter 10
FREE WILL

Tenth Commandment: *Thou Shalt Change*

Between 2003 and 2012, Csanad Szegedi was a leader in the radical far-right Jobbik party of the Hungarian Parliament, notorious for his anti-Semitism. In June of 2012, he revealed that he had just learned that his maternal grandparents were Jewish, and therefore he was a Jew. Szegedi also learned his grandmother had survived Auschwitz.

This dramatic revelation led Szegedi to explore his Jewish roots, and he began to meet with a rabbi. In August 2012, Szegedi apologized to the rabbi for his anti-Semitic remarks and, in 2013, he traveled to Israel where he and his wife visited the Western Wall and Israel's Holocaust museum, *Yad Vashem*. He ultimately decided to embrace his Judaism and adopted the name Dovid, wearing a kipah (skullcap), learning Hebrew, and getting himself circumcised. Szegedi now lives the life of an observant Jew, fully embracing Shabbat and other Jewish practices.

How does one go from being a rabid anti-Semite to fully embracing Judaism? Are people truly capable of that kind of radical change or was this just some fluke of history?

Free Will: Use It or Lose It

The *New York Times* published an article entitled, "Free Will: Now You Have It Now You Don't," which discussed the ongoing debate within the world of science and philosophy as to whether we possess free will. Can humans transcend the repetitive and casual world in which they live and break free of what appear to be controlling factors such as one's socioeconomic and cultural background? Can we act and independently make decisions, or are we merely slaves to our circumstances, be they genetic or environmental?

The world of psychology strongly leans toward the view that we are products of our background and environment and that we cannot, nor should we expect ourselves or others, to go beyond the community and culture in which we are raised. The quintessential American belief that one can go from "rags to riches" seems to remain exclusively within the realm of the economic. It seems that when it comes to virtually everything else, our schools, thought leaders, and counselors teach us that the decisions we make are ultimately predetermined by our family background and by the natural tendencies and dispositions we possess from birth.

Studies seem to indicate this approach is correct. Nicholas H. Wolfinger of the University of Utah concluded that despite the fact that many children of divorced parents vowed not to get divorced themselves, statistically most go through the same experience. Research demonstrates that if one spouse comes from divorced parents the couple is twice as likely to divorce, and spouses who are *both* children of divorced parents are three times as likely to divorce than other couples.[1] Studies show that 80 percent of teens with gambling problems had at least one parent who gambled, and children of alcoholics are four more times likely to become alcoholics themselves.

Judaism for centuries has argued in favor of free will. If classical Judaism stands for anything, it is the fundamental belief that the decisions we make are of our own free will. Our family backgrounds and culture influence those decisions, but they in no way *determine* our choices. Influence yes, determine no.

Maimonides's View

The strongest proponent of this position was the great philosopher and codifier of Jewish law, Maimonides. In his treatise on the Laws of Teshuva (repentance or return), Maimonides takes on the fatalists and extreme astrologists of his time and writes: "Free will is granted to all men. If one desires to turn himself to the path of good and be righteous, the choice is his. Should he desire to turn to the path of evil and be wicked, the choice is his. This is [the intent of] the Torah's statement (Genesis 3:22): 'Behold, man has become unique as ourselves, knowing good and evil,' i.e., the human species became singular in the world with no other species resembling it in the following quality: that man can, on his own initiative, with his knowledge and thought, know good and evil, and do what he desires. There is no one who can prevent him from doing good or bad."[2]

Maimonides continues to say that: "A person should not entertain the thesis held by the fools among the gentiles and the undeveloped among Israel that, at the time of a man's creation, God decrees whether he will be righteous or wicked. This is untrue. Each person is fit to be righteous like Moses, our teacher, or wicked, like Jeroboam. [Similarly,] he may be wise or foolish, merciful or cruel, miserly or generous, or [acquire] any other character traits. There is no one who compels him, sentences him, or leads him towards either of these two paths. Rather, he on his own initiative and decision, tends to the path he chooses . . . This principle is a fundamental concept and a pillar [on which rest the totality] of the Torah and mitzvoth as [Deuteronomy 30:15] states: 'Behold, I have set before you today life [and good, death and evil].' Similarly, [Deuteronomy 11:26] states, 'Behold, I have set before you today [the blessing and the curse],' implying that the choice is in your hands."[3]

Maimonides continues to argue the point, asking why the Almighty would bother to send prophets to exhort his people to follow in His ways if their life decisions were predetermined? What point is there to the entire Torah? Why also would we need or be given a day of atonement, called Yom Kippur, the holiest day on the Jewish calendar, to seek forgiveness for our sins and mistakes? Why should we have to beg forgiveness for anything we've done "wrong" if those actions reflect something predetermined and are not the product of our own free will?

Our Deck of Cards

Maimonides advances a strong argument; however, it seems to run counter to a well-known passage from the Talmud: "For R. Hanina b. Papa made the following exposition: The name of the angel who is in charge of conception is [called] 'Night,' and he takes up a drop [of sperm] and places it in the presence of the Holy One, blessed be He, saying, 'Sovereign of the universe, what shall be the fate of this drop? Shall it produce a strong man or a weak man, a wise man or a fool, a rich man or a poor man?"[4]

If we stopped this reading of the Talmud at this point, it would seem to contradict the belief in free will articulated by Maimonides. Even before a fetus is formed the Talmud implies much of the personality of the child has already been determined! Intelligence, strength, and even financial status all seem to be predetermined.

However, the passage in the Talmud concludes: "but whether the child will be a righteous or evil . . . for everything is in God's hands except for fear of Heaven."[5] "Fear of heaven" refers specifically to the concern a religiously-minded person has that his or her actions are in conformity with God's will, but more generally, it refers to one's value system. *Fear of heaven* is the attitude with which we approach the circumstances of our lives—the values we rely upon to make important decisions. *Not* the circumstances in which we find ourselves but *what* we decide to do with those circumstances—how we deal with the deck of cards which we have been dealt, not the deck itself.

The Talmud is teaching us that we really do not have much control over our life circumstances: what we look like, how smart or foolish we are, or how rich or poor we become. There are of course exceptions, but genetic and socioeconomic factors are primarily at play when it comes to that reality. However, the Talmud teaches that what we choose to do with our reality, with the deck of cards we are dealt, is entirely up to us. *That* is where we have total free will, precisely where it matters. We are not measured, nor would it be fair to be measured, for traits or qualities over which we have no control.

The inspirational Jewish educator, Rebbetzin Esther Jungreis, once remarked: "It doesn't matter whether you are a doctor, lawyer or taxi driver. What matters is *what kind* of doctor, lawyer or car driver you are." As a doctor, are you able to maintain a sense of humility and care not only for the medical condition of your patient but also for his or her feelings? As an attorney, are you placing the needs of your client first, or as a taxi driver do you hand back the right change to your passenger and manage to wish him or her a good day? *Those* decisions are in our hands.

Yes, our socioeconomic background and the influence of our family and friends determines in part what careers we choose, but *what we do* with that career and the values we apply to the issues which arise every day in our jobs is entirely in our hands. *That is* where we have a choice, and as far as Judaism is concerned, that is the only realm that truly matters in life. We may obsess over how much money we make or what we look like, but the Torah cares more about ethics and morality, and how we act when confronted with difficult choices. That's why we believe God gave us the Torah: not to change our reality but to learn how to deal with it. Rather than focusing on improving our existence, on making more money or changing our looks, what is more important is to know how to approach our reality.

And no one can take that power from us. The well-known existential psychiatrist and Holocaust survivor, Victor Frankel, wrote in his *Man's Search for Meaning* that this was precisely what the Nazis were trying to prove in the concentration camps: that if you sufficiently reduce the dignity of a person, you can strip him or her of their free will. Part of the Nazis' virulent evil was to manipulate a prisoner's circumstances to force them into subhuman acts. Frankel said that every time a Jew gave up his or her rations to help someone else in the camps, they proved the Nazis wrong. He said, "We who lived in concentration camps can remember the men who walked through the huts comforting others, giving away their last piece of bread. They may have been few in number but they offer sufficient proof that everything can be taken from a man but one thing: the last of the human freedoms—to choose one's attitude in any given set of circumstances."[6]

But compared to the reality itself, does the way we handle those circumstances make such a difference? If we can't control the *what* of our lives, the stuff that happens to us, then does the *how* or the way we deal with the situation really matter?

Yes, indeed—the way we handle a situation can make all the difference. Look at Dr. Rachamim Melamed Cohen who, at the age of fifty-seven, had a great life. The father of six beautiful children and a proud grandfather, Dr. Cohen held a senior position in the Israeli Ministry of Education and had published two critically acclaimed books. One day he began to feel some weakness in his left shoulder and when he made Kiddush on Shabbat evening, the Kiddush cup shook and the wine spilled. Dr. Cohen and his wife Elisheva began to visit numerous specialists before one doctor told him he had Lou Gehrig's Disease. The doctor outlined the relentless and fatal course of the disease. Cohen would become paralyzed and, in the final stage, his lungs would stop working. "You will become dependent on other people for everything," the doctor told him. "You have three to five years to live."

That was fifteen years ago. Since that time, although Rachamim Cohen has become completely paralyzed and can only communicate through a program which tracks his eye movement, he still begins his day by praying and studying Torah. He continues to go to work where he is consulted by people throughout the world on a myriad of educational issues. Dr. Cohen has mastered Photoshop software, which allows him to paint with his eyes, and has debated Israeli advocates of euthanasia in public. Most incredibly, since his illness, Rachamim Cohen has authored eight new books, with subjects ranging from education to Jewish topics to poetry and a book of advice for people suffering from chronic or terminal illnesses.

How does a person whose life is so profoundly compromised function so highly? Because Rachamim Cohen invests his energies, not in changing his reality over which he has little control, but on what he *can* do. His efforts are focused not on the deck of cards he has been dealt, but on playing those cards in the most advantageous manner to his situation.

On a more philosophical level, the *way* we deal with the circumstances of our lives ultimately develops us into the people we are meant to be. The *Ramchal*, Rabbi Moshe Chaim Luzzatto, a great eighteenth-century Kabbalist and philosopher, in his brilliant work *The Way of God* wrote that each of us is presented with certain traits or qualities which need to be developed in a way so as to enable us to grow and self-actualize. Our life circumstances and the stuff that happens to us, depending on how we handle them, challenge us to develop those traits in one way or another. For example, suggests the *Ramchal*, the life circumstances of wealth and poverty exist to provide an opportunity to demonstrate generosity or indifference. The wealthy are tested to see if they will be generous to the plight of the poor, and the poor are tested to see if they can become satisfied with the little they possess. "Every man's predicament in life is, therefore, his challenge" and each of us is confronted with a certain set of circumstances necessary for our perfection.[7] Every individual's life circumstances are different because each person requires a different set of challenges to enable that person to actualize his or her unique potential. Whatever deck of cards life deals you defines the circumstances you must confront to develop into the very best version of yourself. It's a question of how you use those circumstances to shape your destiny.

Again, upbringing and genetics play an influential role, but they are not determinants. No matter our background, the gene pool from which we are born, or how we've lived our lives until now, we can break from patterns and habits and make our own decision to change.

No person makes this point more dramatically than Larry Trapp.

The Cantor and the Klansman

In 1991, Cantor Michael Weisser and his wife, Julie, moved to Lincoln, Nebraska, where Michael was to assume the Cantor position at the local synagogue, Congregation Bnei Jeshurun. As Cantor Michael and Julie were unpacking boxes, the phone rang and the voice on the other end said slowly and loudly: "You will be sorry you ever moved in [to that house], Jew boy!" The line went dead. Two days later, the Weissers received a thick brown packet in the mail with a card on top that read, "The KKK is watching you, scum." The Weissers called the police, who said the hate mail looked like the work of Larry Trapp, the state leader of the Ku Klux Klan. Also an avowed Nazi, Trapp was suspected of leading skinheads and Klansmen in terrorizing African-American, Vietnamese, and Jewish families in Nebraska and Iowa.

Although Larry Trapp was a diabetic and in a wheelchair, his hate was extraordinary. He was a major Midwestern link in the national white supremacist movement responsible for the fire-bombings of several African-American homes around Lincoln and the burning of the Indochinese Refugee Assistance Center in Omaha. At the time, he was making plans to bomb B'nai Jeshurun, the synagogue where Michael Weisser had just become Cantor.

Michael and Julie were understandably concerned, but did not want to feel like victims. They decided to start calling Trapp on the phone in Nebraska. Michael called several times just to keep the line busy, but then began to leave his own messages. "Larry," he said. "Why do you hate me? You don't even know me." Another time: "Larry, do you know that the first laws the Nazis passed were against people like yourself who had physical deformities, handicaps? Do you realize you would have been among the first to die under Hitler? Why do you love the Nazis so much?"

Michael just kept calling, leaving messages. One night he asked his wife: "What will I do if the guy ever picks up the phone?"

"Tell him you want to do something nice for him," she said. "Tell him you'll take him to the grocery store or something; anything to help him. It will catch him off guard."

One day, just as Michael was leaving another message, Larry, increasingly annoyed by the calls, picked up the phone and shouted, "What the [blank] do you want?"

"I just want to talk to you," said Michael.

"Why the [blank] are you harassing me? Stop harassing me!" Larry yelled.

"I don't want to harass you," Michael replied. "I just want to talk to you."

"I know your voice. You black by any chance?" Larry asks.

"No, I'm Jewish, I'm actually the Cantor at the local synagogue."

"You're harassing me," said Larry. "What do you want? Make it quick."

Remembering his wife's advice, Michael responded, "I was thinking you might need a hand with something, and I wondered if I could help. I know you're in a wheelchair and I thought maybe I could take you to the grocery store or something."

Silence.

Larry couldn't think of anything to say. He cleared his throat and, when he spoke, his voice sounded calmer. "That's okay," Larry said. "That's nice of you, but I've got that covered. Thanks anyway. But don't call this number anymore."

Before he could hang up, Michael replied, "I'll be in touch."

Michael's calls were making Larry confused, and other things were happening to him as well. He received a letter from a former nurse in Lincoln, who wrote: "If you give your love to God, like you gave yourself to the KKK, He'll heal you of all that bitterness, hatred and hurt . . . " Then, at a visit to his eye doctor, Larry felt his wheelchair moving. "I helping you on elevator," a young female voice behind him said. He asked where she was from. "I from Vietnam," she said. That evening, he began to cry as he thought about the scent of the woman's gardenia perfume, his memories of his service in Vietnam, and his assaults on the Vietnamese community.

"I'm rethinking a few things," he told Michael in a subsequent phone call. But a few days later he was back on TV, shrieking about "kike," "half-breeds," and "the Jewish media." Furious, Michael called Larry, who answered his phone. "It's clear you're not rethinking anything at all," Michael said, demanding an explanation.

Larry apologized: "I'm sorry I did that. I've been talking like that all of my life . . . I can't help it . . . I'll apologize."

Around dinnertime the next day, the Weisser's phone rang. "I want to get out," Larry said, "but I don't know how." Michael asked Larry if he and Julie could go over to his apartment to talk in person. Larry hesitated but then finally agreed.

When the door to Larry's apartment creaked open, Michael and Julie saw the bearded Larry Trapp in his wheelchair. An automatic weapon was slung over the doorknob and a Nazi flag hung on the wall. Michael took Larry's hand, and he broke into tears. He looked down at his two silver swastika rings. "Here," he said, yanking them off his fingers and putting them in Michael's hand. "I can't wear these anymore. Will you take them away?" Michael and Julie looked at each other in stunned silence.

Larry began to cry. "I'm so sorry for all the things I've done," he said. Michael and Julie put their arms around Larry and hugged him. Overwhelmed by emotion, they started crying, too.

On November 16, 1991, Larry resigned from the Klan and soon quit all his other racist organizations. He wrote apologies to the many people he had threatened or abused. "I wasted forty years of my life and caused harm to other people," Larry wrote.

On the next New Year's Eve, Larry learned he had less than a year to live. That night, the Weissers invited him to move into their home, and he came. They converted their living room into his bedroom. As his health deteriorated, Julie quit her job to care for him. She fed him and waited on him in his sickness, sometimes all through the night.

Having a remorseful, dying Klansman in their home was disruptive to the whole family, which included three teenagers, a dog, and a cat, but everyone pitched in. On days when Larry was well enough, he listened to speeches by the Reverend Martin Luther King and read books on Gandhi. Living in a Cantor's home, Larry was surrounded by Jewish paraphernalia and Jewish music. He started to read books on Judaism and began to explore the Jewish faith. Little by little Larry developed a keen interest in Judaism and spent many hours a day studying.

On June 5, 1992, Larry Trapp converted to Judaism in ceremonies at B'nai Jeshurun, the very synagogue he had planned to blow up! Three months later, on September 6, 1992, Larry died in the Weisser home, with Michael and Julie beside him, holding his hands.

A man whose entire life was filled with hate and hostility for Jews and so many others, with the help of some very special people, was able to rid himself of hate and became a different person. Even though Larry spent the first forty years of his life one way, eventually he made a real change and spent his last years as a different person.[8]

When it comes to our attitude or our values, we *always* have a choice. Our family background and the environment in which we are raised influence, but they do not determine, the values we decide for ourselves. It's those values and attitude which ultimately define who we are—not our professions, not our looks, not the money, not all the things which are fixed and less determined by our choices. We are the choices we make and those choices are based on what we and we alone decide is right or wrong. That's what makes us human and that will always remain in our hands.

That is why Judaism believes so much in change and why the Jewish faith devotes so much time to this enterprise. The Jewish calendar each year starts with the Hebrew month of *Elul*, in which God is believed to be spiritually closer and during which time we work on our character through extra praying and more Torah study. Rosh Hashana, the official beginning of the Jewish year, then presents the opportunity for the community to come together for prayer and introspection and to hear the sounds of the shofar which are intended to wake us up to correct our wrongs and become better people. That is then followed by ten days of soul-searching and asking forgiveness of anyone we may have wronged, culminating in Yom Kippur, the holiest day of the Jewish year, when we engage in the most intense form of "teshuva," or returning to our true selves, by making good on the mistakes and sins we've committed, cleansing ourselves, and emerging purified after this intense twenty-four-hour period of fasting and deep introspection.

The Torah mandates all this because it so strongly believes we are capable of change. If Larry Trapp could leave the KKK and his hateful ways, each of us can transform ourselves in whatever way we choose. The important question is never what kind of life we somehow got used to living yesterday, but what kind of life we commit ourselves to building tomorrow.

In one of the most stirring and poetic prayers of the Yom Kippur liturgy, the great rabbinic liturgist Eliezer Hakalir authored the famous prayer, "Behold we are like clay in the hand of the Potter." This Piyut (poetic prayer) is commonly understood as expressing humankind's utter helplessness before God: "We are clay in God's hand." However, if you look at the part of the Prophets from where the author Hakalir derives this phrase, namely Jeremiah chapter 18, you see a very different picture: God tells Jeremiah the prophet to go down to the house of the potter and from there the prophet will hear the Almighty's word. Jeremiah goes to the potter's house and God tells him: " . . . behold as clay in the potter's hand so are you in My hand, O House of Israel. In one instant I may speak about a nation and concerning a kingdom, to uproot and to demolish and to destroy. And when that nation repents of its evil for which I spoke concerning it, I will repent the evil that I thought to do it."[9] This verse teaches that even if God planned to punish a nation for acting evil, but the nation changes its ways for the good, God will "repent the evil He thought to do," namely, God will change his whole approach to that nation. And conversely as the prophesy continues: "In one instant I will speak concerning a kingdom to build and to plant. And it will do what is evil in MY eyes, not to hearken to MY voice, I will repent of the good I said to benefit."[10] This passage means that if God was going to help to build up a nation but that nation begins to act in an evil way, again God will change His whole approach. Thus, we might think we are just clay in God's hands, objects to be manipulated with no ability to make our own decisions or shape our own destinies, but it's just the opposite. God acts or reacts according to *our* actions. God responds and deals with us depending on what *we* decide to do!

The famous story involving Adam's two sons, Cain and Abel, echoes this teaching. Each brings an offering to God: Cain brings an offering from the fruit of the ground and Abel from the best of his flock. God responds positively to Abel's offering, but turns away from Cain's. Cain gets angry and becomes despondent and God says to him: "Why are you annoyed and why has your countenance fallen? Surely if you improve yourself, you will be forgiven. But if you do not improve, sin rests at the door. Its desire is toward you but you can conquer it."[11] You have the power to act, to make your own choices. We have the power to choose and determine how we want to live our lives. Yes, we have strong influences—our family background and our society—and those influences impact the decisions we make, but ultimately, we get to choose how to live.

Old Habits Die Hard

But let's face it, most of us usually just go with what's familiar and comfortable. We conform to what we've been trained to do and the longer we remain in that state, the harder it is to break out. There's a famous myth involving frogs and hot water. If a frog is placed in boiling water, it will of course jump out; but if it is placed in cold water and that cold water is very gradually heated up, the frog will not perceive the danger and will remain in the water until its death. While that is just a myth, we humans do the same thing. The longer we remain in a certain place or get used to thinking or behaving in a certain fixed way, the more difficult it is for us to break the pattern. The great Jewish thinker, Rabbi Yehudah Halevi, wrote in one of his poems: "The world at large is a prison and every man is a prisoner." We trap ourselves with our own self-imposed limitations and by the habits and behaviors that we blindly follow. According to the Society for Personality and Social Psychology, as many as 40 percent of our daily activities are driven by habit. Habit dictates the way we eat, the way we diet and exercise (or don't exercise), the way we spend our free time; we follow what we've always done or what everyone else is doing. And you can see it in the realm of religious observance maybe more than anywhere else: We confine ourselves by the labels we place on ourselves and each other, usually based on the way we were raised. When I've suggested to some who only attend MJE's High Holiday services that they also come and check out our Shabbat services, I've heard people respond: "Rabbi, I'm only a once- or twice-a-year Jew." Or when I've encouraged others who come every Shabbat to come to services on time, I've heard: "Never before 11 a.m., rabbi" (services start at 9:30) or "Rabbi, I'm a JFKer"—Just for Kiddush (refreshments after the service).

"Keep Believing in Yourself"

We can choose to break out of the box, to release ourselves from the prison in which we've confined ourselves. Once we realize the habits we practice hold us back, we know we're capable of so much more, but that requires us to believe in ourselves. There's a story told of a professor who stood before his class of thirty senior molecular biology students, about to pass out the final exam. "I have been privileged to be your instructor this semester, and I know how hard you have all worked to prepare for this test. I also know most of you are off to medical school or grad school next fall," the professor said to the class. "I am well aware of how much pressure you are under to keep your GPAs up, and because I know you are all capable of understanding this material, I am prepared to offer an automatic B to anyone who would prefer not to take the final." The relief was audible. Several students jumped up to thank the professor and departed from class. The professor looked at the handful of students who remained, and offered again, "Any other takers? This is your last opportunity." One more student decided to go. Seven students remained. The professor closed the door and took attendance. Then he handed out the final exam.

There were two sentences typed on the exam paper: "Congratulations, you have just received an A in this class. Keep believing in yourself."

If we truly believe in ourselves, we will perform better. We can transform ourselves.

We can change. If someone who lived a life of hating for so many years can rid himself of anger, we can rise above our bad habits and start being kinder, gentler people. We can put the needs and feelings of our co-workers, our parents, and our friends before ourselves. We're not selfish people. We may feel that way and we may even act that way at times, but we can change and rise above it. As God told Cain: "Its desire is toward you but you can conquer it."[12]

We can be more serious about our spiritual lives and start studying and praying more. We can donate more money to people in need or to causes in which we believe. It's just a question of what we think we're capable of and how much we want to grow.

We only get one shot at life: let's make sure we don't sell ourselves short by not expecting more from ourselves today than we did yesterday. Today is a new day and since change is possible, we can do better. "Im tirzeh, ain zo agada," said the legendary founder of Zionism Theodore Herzl. "If you will it, it will not remain a dream."

Notes

1. "Research Suggests Children of Divorce More Likely to End Their Own Marriages," June 27, 2005, https://archive.unews.utah.edu/news_releases/research-suggests-children -of-divorce-more-likely-to-end-their-own-marriages/.
2. Maimonides, Mishnah Torah, Laws of Repentance 5:1.
3. Ibid, 5:2,3.
4. Talmud, Niddah 16b.
5. Ibid.
6. Victor Frankel, *Man's Search for Meaning* (New York: Simon & Schuster, 1984), 86.
7. Rabbi Moshe Chaim Luzzatto, *The Way of God* (Nanuet, NY: Philipp Feldheim, 2009), 111.

8. Jack Canfield, Mark Victor Hansen, and Dov Peretz Elkins, *Chicken Soup for the Jewish Soul* (Deerfield Beach, FL: HCI, 2001).
9. Jeremiah 18:6–8.
10. Jeremiah 18:9,10.
11. Genesis 4:6,7.
12. Ibid.

EPILOGUE

Eleventh Commandment: *Don't Let the Perfect Be the Enemy of the Good*

While there were only *ten* commandments (besides the remaining 603 expressed in the Torah) revealed at Sinai, after which this book was modeled, I want to leave you with one more: an eleventh commandment which I believe necessary to finding success in applying the first ten.

There's a story told of a man who joins a monastery and takes a vow of silence: he's only allowed to say two words every seven years. After the first seven years, the elders bring him in and ask for his two words. "Cold floors," he says. They nod and send him away. Seven more years pass. They bring him back in and ask for his two words. He clears his throats and says, "Bad food." They nod and send him away. Seven more years pass. They bring him in for his two words. "I quit," he says.

"That's not surprising," the elders say. "You've done nothing but complain since you got here."

I share this obviously true story with you because even in a monastery where things are supposed to be simple and *perfect*, it's never the case. There's always something we can find to complain about because life is never perfect. Dealing with perfectionism is the eleventh lesson with which I'd like to leave you, since it pertains to each of the previous ten lessons and remains an issue with which I and many others struggle.

Ever since I can remember I've had a strong desire for things to be perfect—to look just right. As a child before going to sleep each night I'd make sure my slippers were perfectly aligned with my bed. I remember being bothered when someone would come into my room and mess them up, usually my brother. I wanted those slippers perfectly lined up. I was one of those kids who would spend hours arranging my blocks in such a way that every block had its proper place, only to see it knocked down (usually again by my brother who really disliked my perfectionism). I rebelled for a while during my gap year in Israel and continued my rebellion in college when I roomed with some pretty messy guys (great guys, just real slobs), but to this day, I continue to be acutely aware of the small things that are often missing—a fork at someone's table setting, a bulb in the corner of the room that burned out, a tile missing on the wall. There's no question that much of this is pure "meshuga'as," or craziness as they say in Yiddish. There's even a psychological term for my obsessive-compulsive behavior. They call it the *Missing Tile Syndrome.* However, I've always felt (or maybe just hoped) that there was something deeper to this compulsion, a desire for all things and all people to be perfect. Of course, what often comes with that desire is a sense that if whatever project you're working on will never be perfect, if it will never look like it ideally should, then why bother at all?

This is not a healthy attitude to have as far as Judaism is concerned. When God first approached Moses at the scene of the burning bush and asked him to lead the Jewish people out of Egyptian slavery, Moses reacted with great hesitancy. "Who am I to go before Pharaoh?" Moses asks God.[1] Later he says: "I'm not a man of words . . . I am slow of speech and slow of tongue."[2] Moses explains he's not the right man for the job because he is imperfect; after all, he argues, he has a speech impediment. Moses seems to be offering a valid reason. Isn't it important for the one person representing the Jewish people before Pharaoh to be able to speak properly? Can you imagine the United States appointing someone with a speech impediment to represent its interests to another government? However, God dismisses Moses's hesitancy by saying, " . . . go and I will be with your mouth and I will teach you what to say."[3]

Still though, Moses was not satisfied: "Please my Master, send the person you really want to send."[4] God then gets angry with Moses dragging his feet and tells him to take his brother Aaron to help him before Pharaoh.

This back and forth between God and Moses goes on for some time; it's the longest dialogue in the whole Bible, actually. But why? Why was Moses so reticent about accepting his role as leader? Why would he doubt God's choice and his own ability to carry out his divinely-given mission?

Some of the biblical commentators (Sforno and Ramban) explain that Moses simply could not believe God would choose as his messenger someone whose glaring deficiencies made him less than perfect for the job. Moses implored God to send someone who *was* perfect. Why not choose someone with better qualifications? Someone He wouldn't have to help all the time. Send someone else, Moses was saying, because I'm too far from perfect. God's reaction: I know about your speech problem and it's okay. I'll get you some help but you will be just fine. I don't need someone perfect. I want you just as you are.

God was teaching a vital teaching: not everything in life needs to be perfect for it to be good. Moses had compassion and dedication. He had courage and empathy as evidenced by his defending of a Jewish Hebrew slave being beaten by an Egyptian taskmaster. He had a lot of the qualities to be God's messenger—he didn't have them *all* but he had enough.

Our society celebrates perfection particularly when it comes to external things, like the way we look and how we sound, but there's a danger in this—the danger of not being able to see the blessings we *do* have in our lives.

The Grace After Meals, the blessings we say after eating a meal, contains four blessings. The first three blessings are biblically mandated by Moses, Joshua, and David, whereas the fourth blessing, that "God is good and does good," was instituted by the rabbinic sages after the

Roman massacre in the Jewish city of Beitar.[5] Beitar was the last stronghold of the Bar Kochva revolt against the Romans. In the aftermath of the second Temple destruction, the Jews held out against the Roman legions for many years, but eventually the Romans defeated the Jewish army and killed hundreds of thousands of Beitar's inhabitants, denying the Jewish people the basic right to bury their brethren. Approximately seven years later, after much praying and fasting, as well as bribing the Roman despots, the Jews were finally granted permission to bury those who were killed. When the Jews were allowed back to bury the slain, the bodies had somehow not decomposed, even after all those years. A miracle took place—the bodies remained preserved and the slain of Beitar were given a proper burial. That miracle inspired the Jewish Sages to institute the blessing of "God is good and does good" within the Grace After Meals, recited by millions of Jews to this day.

What a strange incident over which to recite a blessing! Why would the sages ordain a blessing over the fact that that the slain of Beitar were finally able to receive a proper burial? How can a blessing be instituted after something so tragic?

The Jewish Sages were telling us that even a partial good is worthy of celebration, that even something which is bitter deserves a word of praise if there's also something good to it. Something does not have to be perfect for it to warrant a blessing. Just as God selected Moses, speech impediment and all, the Jewish Sages looked out at an imperfect world and found reason to recite a blessing, because even the imperfect can be good.

The question is whether *we* can do this in our own lives. Are we able to say a blessing over something good when it's not great? How many such blessings have we been given in our lives? How many truly *good* things have happened to us that we've written off because they could have been better? How many *good* relationships, because they weren't *great* relationships, because they weren't perfect, did we let go? I often wonder how many of those relationships could have been good marriages, but never made it to that point because the interaction was just good but not spectacular.

Hollywood has done a number on us. The perfect image of relationships that movies portray has found its way into our subconscious, blurring fantasy and reality. We imagine the idyllic romance of two picture perfect people on a movie screen. We forget that just a few feet in front of them are lights, cameras, and a director managing each actor's every move. We meet someone whose company we enjoy, whose values we respect, but we're so convinced that nothing less than the kind of bliss these films portray will make us happy, we dismiss them in the hope of finding something better. Please don't misunderstand me: I enjoy movies and I believe in love, but love is never perfect. Love between two people that isn't perfect is still love.

The same lesson goes for the qualities we look for in a mate: The Talmud tells us that a father should always endeavor to have his daughter marry a Torah scholar. If that's not possible, the Talmud continues, then the father should try to marry his daughter to someone known for doing good deeds. If that's not possible, says the Talmud, then to one who helps run the local synagogue. If not, then to the person who collects and distributes charity, and if not him, then to the one who teaches Torah to the children in the community.[6]

The Talmud recognizes that ideally, we may be looking for certain qualities in a partner, but if we can't seem to find exactly what we're looking for, it's okay to look for something else, a *different* positive attribute. I once heard a story of a young woman who had her mind set on marrying an accountant. It wasn't anything special about accountants per se, but the woman wanted to marry a professional with what she perceived as more of a nine-to-five type of job. In any event, the local matchmaker received a phone call about a certain man who the matchmaker thought was a great idea for this woman. The only problem was he was not an accountant—he was a rabbi! When the young woman called to ask the matchmaker if the man was an accountant, the matchmaker lied and said yes. (Not saying I approve of the matchmaker's response, but that's what happened.) The couple went out on a date and they immediately clicked. They went out a few times and by the time the woman found out the man she was dating was a rabbi and not an accountant, she was already smitten. They got married and thirty years later they are now known as one of the most dynamic rabbinic couples in the country.

I quoted John Lennon in an earlier chapter: "Life is what happens to you while you're busy making other plans." We can't plan everything and sometimes sticking to *the plan*, to everything we think we need to be happy, can be the biggest mistake. So often we find happiness in situations or in other people who lack what we thought was necessary for our personal happiness. Our perceived need for perfection can truly become the enemy of the good.

The same goes for our spiritual lives. Here too the perfect can prevent us from having the good. One of my students interested in observing the Sabbath once asked me, "If I don't observe the entire Sabbath the way it's ideally *supposed* to be practiced, does it pay to do it all?" Another student expressed an interest in observing the Jewish dietary laws, but was reluctant to do so since she wasn't also Sabbath observant. "Isn't it hypocritical to do one and not the other?" she questioned. I told her it would of course be ideal to do both, but one is certainly better then neither. Start with one, feel good about that, and don't let the perfect be the enemy of the good.

The late Prime Minister of Israel, Ariel Sharon, was a great Jewish hero both on the battlefield and in Israeli politics, but not necessarily a religious personality. After the terrible Sbarro's pizzeria terrorist bombing in Jerusalem in 2001, Prime Minister Sharon went to the hospital to visit the surviving children of a Jewish Dutch family, whose parents were killed in the attack. When Sharon asked one of the children if there was anything he could do for him, the little boy asked if the Prime Minister would observe the following Shabbat in memory of his parents. Sharon was taken aback by the request, but promised he would try. The Prime Minister kept his word. The next weekend he refrained from his usual round of official business and politics—he took no phone calls and did not travel. Sure, the ideal is to observe Shabbat every week, but one Shabbat is also special.

Every positive action we take, every act of spirituality and goodness we initiate has value, even if it's far from the ideal, because things don't have to be perfect to be good—a teaching rooted in the very fabric of creation. In our prayers recited at the end of the holy day of Yom Kippur, we turn to God and say: "You set man apart from the very beginning and you considered him worthy to stand before You."[7] The sage, the Avudraham, in his comments on the Jewish prayers, explains that this prayer refers to the first man, Adam, who God "set apart" or removed from the Garden of Eden because of his sin and imperfections. Yet, as the prayer continues: "you considered him worthy to stand before You," meaning, after expelling Adam and Eve from Eden, humankind was still worthy to stand before God, as the Almighty allowed them to live in proximity to Eden. Adam's and Eve's imperfections may have made them unworthy to live *in* paradise, but they were still worthy of living *close* to paradise.

This is the dialectical relationship God has with humanity. Like any parent, God had high hopes for his children. When that ideal was not realized, when Adam and Eve failed to live up to God's original plan, the Almighty didn't simply dispense with them and the whole project of creation. He changed the plan, found them a more suitable place to live, and began to love them for who they were. Like *any* parent whose high hopes and dreams for their child exceed the reality, God set that vision of perfection aside and still considered humanity worthy to stand before Him. We don't need to be perfect to have a relationship with our Creator. Good is good enough.

And so, in applying any of the ten commandments I've shared in this book, please remember—it's not an all-or-nothing game. If, for example, as I shared in the first chapter, you want to find greater happiness through giving to others, you don't need to quit your job, break up with your significant other, and join the Peace Corps. Within your everyday life, there are people who need help. Take some time out of your schedule to help them. Find a cause in which you believe and commit once a week to do some volunteering. Visit someone who is elderly and alone in your neighborhood. Try stretching yourself to give more charity. If you can't manage to donate the ten percent of your annual income (after taxes) which Jewish tradition teaches, then donate five percent. Three percent. One percent. Whatever you can afford is better than nothing.

In chapter 9, I spoke about the Jewish traditions of the Sabbath and Blessings as ways of becoming more present and aware. To observe those traditions fully one must be very disciplined. In the case of blessings, it means saying a blessing before and after you eat anything. Observing the Sabbath in an ideal manner also requires great discipline, refraining from the thirty-nine "work" activities of which we spoke. If these observances seem too daunting to practice in full, then do some of them. Refrain from *some* of the Shabbat labors each week, say a blessing over *some* of the foods you eat. Maybe it's not the ideal, but it's still a positive step forward which will probably inspire you to do more. As Ben Azzai, a sage of the Mishnaic period, famously said: "For a mitzvah brings another mitzvah."[8] When you do one good thing it usually turns into another.

And so in conclusion, try your best to apply the lessons I've shared in this book, but while doing so, don't let the perfect become the enemy of the good. As a good rabbi should, let me leave you with a blessing based on what I shared in this book.

Give to other people and be sure not to be too focused on yourself.

Commit to one other person, and, together, elevate the physical around you.

Learn to be okay with failing for it is the only way to grow.

Believe in yourself, but take responsibility for your actions, never shifting the blame to others.

Be proactive, and try not to play the victim.

Have a specific mission in life, and always choose what's right over what's popular.

Try to look up and not just around when making important decisions.

Celebrate the journey.

Know that real change is possible.

And don't let the perfect become the enemy of the good.